A CALL TO OBSERVE

In His Hand is the Life of Every Living Thing

By
James R. Bjorge

Kirk House Publishers
Minneapolis, Minnesota

A Call to Observe
In His Hand is the Life of Every Living Thing
by James R. Bjorge

Photography courtesy of Leonard Flachman

Library of Congress Cataloging-In-Publication Data
Bjorge, James R.
    A call to observe : in His hand is the life of every living thing / by James R.
    Bjorge.
        p.cm.
        ISBN 1-886513-75-9
        1. Creation—Meditations. 2. Nature—Religious aspects—Christianity. 3.
    Devotional calendars. I. Title.
    BT695.5 .B55 2002
    242—dc21
                                                        2002030056

Kirk House Publishers, PO Box 390759, Minneapolis, MN 55439
Manufactured in the United States of America

DEDICATION

To my wife, Fran
1934-2002
You are, and always will be,
My gift from God...
The love of my life.
Jim

To my grandson, Willy
1993-2002
In the words of George MacDonald,
He was a "gleam-faced, pure-eyed, strong-willed, high-hearted boy,"
with so much future before him.

In thankfulness for the Ministry of Mount Carmel Bible Camp
which is a special place in the life of the Bjorge family.

In His hand
is the life
of every living thing
and the
breath of all mankind
Job 12:10

Table Of Contents

PREFACE

Job describes God's mystery and sovereignty in this way: "But ask the beasts, and they will teach you; the birds of the air, and they will tell you; or the plants of the earth, and they will teach you; and the fish of the sea will declare to you. Who among these does not know that the hand of the Lord has done this? In his hand is the life of every living thing and the breath of all mankind" (Job 12:7-10).

In the Psalms, David reminds us that God speaks to us through two books: the masterpiece of creation and, of course, directly through the written Word of God. "The heavens are telling the glory of God; and the firmament proclaims his handiwork. Day to day pours forth speech, and night to night declares knowledge" (Psalm 19:1-2). The apostle Paul clearly tells us that God speaks through the natural world: "Ever since the creation of the world his invisible nature, namely, his eternal power and deity, has been clearly perceived in the things that have been made. So they are without excuse" (Romans 1:20).

Jesus was very much aware of his Father's world, and thus employed illustrations from nature for his teachings. The vines and the trees, fish and birds, seeds, sheep and shepherds were woven into his discourses.

By observing God's wonderful world of nature we will be led to worship the Creator.

Henry van Dyke expressed it well in his hymn, "Joyful, Joyful We Adore Thee." The tune is from Beethoven's "Ninth Symphony".

All Thy works with joy surround Thee,
Earth and heaven reflect Thy rays,
Stars and angels sing around Thee,
Center of unbroken praise.
Field and forest, vale and mountain,

Flowery meadow, flashing sea,
Chanting bird and flowing fountain,
Call us to rejoice in Thee.

May this book ignite some thoughts and provoke reflection as you marvel at God's handiwork in creation.

Never lose an opportunity of seeing anything that is beautiful, for beauty is God's handwriting—a wayside sacrament, welcome it in every fair face, in every fair flower, and thank God for it as a cup of blessing.

– Ralph Waldo Emerson

Nature Belongs to God

Make a joyful noise to God, all the earth; sing the glory of his name; give to him glorious praise! . . . All the earth worships thee; they sing praises to thee (Psalm 66:1-2,4).

Creation was crafted by the mind and will of God, and after every act in the creation story God "saw that it was good." Consequently, if I truly love and praise God, I will also love his wonderful world. To fail to be alive to the beauty of water, sky, and green grass is to fail in our love to God. Robert Louis Stevenson once prayed that the Celestial Surgeon would stab his spirit awake to his books, his food, and summer rain.

A Puritan was once walking with a friend through the forest. As the friend stopped to admire a lovely wildflower, the Puritan said, "I have learned to call nothing lovely in this lost and sinful world." I don't know where he learned that, but I do know it was not from Scripture.

The doctrine of creation placed God as the owner and sustainer of it all. "For every beast of the forest is mine, the cattle on a thousand hills. I know all the birds of the air, and all that moves in the field is mine . . . for the world and all that is in it is mine" (Psalm 50:10-12). His fingerprints are left on the flowers of the field and the sands of the seas. Alfred Tennyson (1809-1892) bathed in the mystery of God's creation. He wrote:

> Flower in the crannied wall,
> I pluck you out of the crannies,
> I hold you here, root and all, in my hand,
> Little flower—but if I could understand
> What you are, root and all, and all in all,
> I should know what God and man is.

Jesus was very much aware of his Father's world. He spoke tenderly of the lilies of the field and the birds of the air. He was aware of the sower going forth with good seed. He ate the grain of the field with thanksgiving and turned water into wine at the wedding in Canna. He rode the waves on the Sea of Galilee and hiked into the hills to pray. His roots, for thirty-three years, penetrated the rocky soil of Palestine.

For seventy years I have been privileged to explore the great out-of-doors from childhood to adulthood. I have always endeavored to see lessons that might spring forth from nature. "But ask the beasts, and they will teach you; the birds of the air, and they will tell you; or the plants of the earth, and they will teach you; and the fish of the sea will declare to you" (Job 12:7-8). Elizabeth Barrett Browning captured this expectant mood in her verse:

Earth's crammed with heaven,
And every common bush afire with God.
But only he who sees takes off his shoes -
The rest sit around and pluck blackberries.

My mother died in 1979 after a second vicious stroke. After her first stroke a year and a half earlier, she was confined to a nursing home. One day while visiting her she asked me to repot one of her plants in the window area. In the process I spilled some of the dirt on the table, and Mom proceeded to scoop it up with her one good hand. I quickly told her I would do it. She responded, "Jim, I like the feel of garden dirt. I don't get to touch it much anymore." Beautiful!

Mom always loved creation, and her large flower gardens were a testimony to that.

Dietrich Bonhoeffer said, "The earth which nourishes me has a rightful claim on my work and energy in return. I have no right to despise the earth on which I live and move. I am bound to it by loyalty and gratitude." The marvels of creation should indeed fill our hearts with gratitude, but always to the Creator.

Creator Lord, may I truly understand that this earth on which I live is your handiwork. May I always be cognizant that nature sings your praise. Help me to take time to look and listen to the wonders your hand has wrought.

Singers Of Life

But about midnight Paul and Silas were praying and singing hymns to God (Acts 16:25).

A person knows spring has arrived when the birds of the air arrive on colored wings from their winter vacation in the south. Upon their return, the trees and bushes on our acreage become the stage for their new concert series. Each bird takes its turn with a thrilling performance which dances in our ears after the solemn stillness of winter.

When all the feathered friends arrive, it occasionally becomes a bedlam of song. The robin scolds the other birds, loudly making her claim to the crotch in the elm tree where she has made plans to build her nest. The little wren explodes with song because she and her mate have found one of our birdhouses to their liking. The songs continue as the winged visitors are filled with joy and anticipation over the new nesting season. The brown thrasher, the oriole, the finches, and numerous others make us thankful for God's gift of birds.

However, into this picture of joy and serenity storm clouds arise even for the innocent birds. A marauding raccoon, in the middle of the night, comes upon the nest of Canadian honkers. After a good fight, the ground is littered with feathers, and the geese retreat and abandon the nest. The raccoon breaks the eggs and has a hearty breakfast before he strolls off along the pond's shore. The hope of little goslings is postponed. A squirrel that decided to eat eggs rather than nuts that day also victimized the robin that built in the crotch of the elm tree. A spring storm, which swept across the prairie, caused our trees to swirl and bend in the fierce gale, and a nest tumbled out of a tall ash tree. The dream of that bird was dashed, and I discovered four small eggs on the ground lying next to the fallen nest.

However, after each disaster the concert of song continued after a short intermission. I recall reading an incident described by anthropologist Loren Eisley. He wrote about watching a huge raven beginning to eat a young bird it has captured. The parent birds fly helplessly overhead, and the air is filled with the protests of many other birds. After a strange silence, a single sparrow hesitantly lifts up a song. Soon it passes from bird to bird until the sky is filled with song. They sing under the brooding shadow of the raven. Eisley states, "In truth they had forgotten the raven, for they were singers of life and not of death."

The birds sang because life is sweet and sunlight is beautiful. They had learned to turn sighs into songs. Such ought to be the life of the church. J. Walter Sylvester said, "Happiness comes not from without but from within. It comes not from the power of possession but from the power of appreciation." The hope that the Risen Christ deposits in our hearts and minds is that which enables us to keep celebrating even in the crucible of disappointment. We, too, are singers of life and not of death.

Two grasshoppers fell into a bowl of cream. One of them complained and groaned over his plight. It was not long before he sank to the bottom and drowned. The other kept singing and cheerfully kicked his legs until the cream turned into butter. He then hopped away to freedom. Life can often be that way if we concentrate more on our blessings. An old Swedish proverb states, "Those who wish to sing can always find a song."

"Let the word of Christ dwell in you richly, teach and admonish one another in all wisdom, and sing psalms and hymns and spiritual songs with thankfulness in your hearts to God" (Colossians 3:16).

Dear Lord, I confess I am more often negative than positive. Criticism surfaces more frequently in my talk than compliments. Put a song in my heart so that my words will lift people up rather than tear them down.

Seed Time

Do not be deceived; God is not mocked, for whatever a man sows, that he will also reap (Galatians 6:7).

The rich black Red River Valley soil had just been turned over by my rotary tiller. It was thoroughly pulverized, then raked smooth. The garden was now ready and begging for seed. I was ready to cooperate as dreams of a summer harvest of vegetables danced in my mind.

First came the potatoes. Several weeks later the seeds of various vegetables were laid to rest in rows. As I was planting, I looked at the seeds of beans, carrots, and beets. In the palm of my hand they were so small, shriveled, and seemingly lifeless. Yet I knew that locked within each seed was a life-giving principle that defies explanation. In time it would produce a body of vegetation, "each according to its kind."

Seeds are mysterious. Some, such as those of the willow, are viable or capable of growing for only a few days after falling from the parent tree. Other seeds are viable for years. Seeds of the Indian lotus have been known to germinate two hundred years after dispersal. The sagebrush plant of the western United States is a dry land plant. Its seed sometimes lies in the earth for ten to fifteen years—dry, dormant, apparently dead, but waiting for a special springtime, a certain season when there will be more than average moisture and conditions will be just right.

One of the amazing facts of the natural world took place in Death Valley during the month of May, 1939. Rain fell for nineteen consecutive days in this lowest, hottest, and driest region of our country. With only a few inches of rain each year, it is a desolate valley of sand dunes. But during that one rainy month, seeds that had been dormant for years sprang to life and parts of the valley became a carpet of beautiful wild flowers. The drab, dry desert was transformed into a flower garden. It was reported that a hundred varieties of flowers were found within a half-hour in one small area.

The life in seeds, waiting to burst forth when the right conditions appear, is a wonderful illustration of the hope that lies hidden within all of us. Isaiah, in his suffering servant chapter, says with awe, "Who has believed what we have heard? And to whom has the arm of the Lord been revealed? For he grew up before him like a young plant, and like a root out of dry ground" (Isaiah 53:1-2).

A root out of dry ground! How often in times of spiritual and emotional dryness we become discouraged, and in those desert years we believe that the qualities of life that we dreamed about are dead and forgotten. Will love blossom again? Will the wonder and awe of childhood be relived? Will bitterness and disappointment ever be erased? Can the shoots of fellowship, joy, and love really grow again?

The answer is "yes." Seeds that may have been planted in you by your parents, Sunday school teachers, and friends may all be waiting for the right conditions in which to sprout and flourish. God wants that to happen. He wants you to keep planting good seed. He is ". . . giving seed to the sower and bread to the eater, so shall my word be that goes forth from my mouth; it shall not return to me empty . . ." (Isaiah 55:10-11).

> Lord, make us instruments of thy peace.
> Where there is hatred, let us sow love;
> Where there is injury, pardon;
> Where there is discord, union;
> Where there is doubt, faith;
> Where there is despair, hope;
> Where there is darkness, light;
> Where there is sadness, joy.
> –(St. Francis of Assisi)

Lord, the words that I speak and the deeds that I do are the seeds that I plant. Help me to be faithful for I know there will be a day of harvest from that which I sowed. Amen.

Importance of Differences

While the earth remains, seedtime and harvest, cold and heat, summer and winter, day and night, shall not cease (Genesis 8:22).

The grip of winter was slowly grinding to a halt. Signs of springtime were evidenced in the arrival of some song birds and the sprouting of green grass. Expectancy was in the air as buds on tree branches were bursting open. Now was the time to visit the nursery and select seeds for the summer garden.

The soil was tilled and raked smooth. The garden was plotted for the various kinds of flowers and vegetables. Then came the time of sowing the seed. On each packet of seeds there were explicit instructions for the most ideal time of the spring for good germination to take place, and also for the depth that the seeds should be placed in the soil. Some seeds should be deposited at one-eighth inch depth, others at one-fourth or one-half inch depths. Upon reading the directions more closely, I discovered that not only the timing and the depth of planting were important, but the type of soil: whether it was sandy or rich loam would make a difference in the health of the growing plant. The amount of moisture was also a consideration. Each seed seemed to have its own preference in the process of planting and germination.

When I was a young boy I had the false notion that the only thing necessary was to stick the seed in the ground at any depth and the result would be the same. How wrong I was! While seeds in many ways are very similar, they need to be treated differently in the planting procedure. People, too, are alike in many ways. They are created in the image of God. God breathed into them the breath of life. But just like seeds, there are different preferences. These differences might seem small, but they are very important.

Personality traits are created by genetics and our environment. The Myers-Briggs Type Indicator is a valuable tool for understanding

personality preferences. No personality is right or wrong, just as being right-handed is no more exalted than being left-handed. And being right-handed does not mean you don't use your left hand.

In American society, introverts are outnumbered by extroverts by about three to one. Therefore, the introverts may have more pressure exerted on them to respond to the majority. The introvert may sometimes appear shy or aloof since he or she is not overly comfortable in groups and receives more energy by being alone or with only one or two others. The extroverts are energized by conversation, and therefore talking and parties stimulate them.

Some people are predominately thinkers, while others are basically feelers. Each group uses its emotional preference in making decisions.

In dealing with people, we must be aware of the differences in the people we encounter and respect those differences. Jesus was always sensitive to the needs and personalities of those to whom he ministered. The Samaritan woman at the well was justly told of both her moral and theological errors. However, Jesus did it in a way that caused no needed embarrassment. Jesus was aware of her loss of dignity, her ostracism from society. From the calling of his disciples to an evening discussion with Nicodemus, Jesus treated people with respect to who they were and from where they were coming in their life journeys.

Charles R. Swindoll said, "God, our wise and creative Maker, has been pleased to make everyone different and no one perfect. The sooner we appreciate and accept the fact, the deeper we will appreciate and accept each other, just as our Designer planned us."

Lord, forgive me for thinking everyone should be like me and enjoy what I enjoy. Curb my selfishness and help me to graciously accept the contributions of various personalities.

A Place of My Own

Then the Lord appeared to Abram, and said "To your descendants I will give this land" (Genesis 12:7a).

One of my favorite birds is the small, plump wren. Its song, composed of a series of musical trills, is a delight to the ears. Since this little bird is so pleasant to watch as it flits and scampers around and is so pleasing to listen to, I've put up several wren houses on our acreage in order to attract them. In the process I've discovered an important truth about birds. Many of them map out their own territory. They simply want a place of their own. Consequently, if two wren houses are placed too close to each other one will be left vacant. The wren which occupies one of the houses establishes an area in which "no trespassing" laws are established. The territory size and spacing varies from one bird species to another. The amount of land a bird claims as its own depends on the food supply and whether the bird is an isolationist or more communal. The bald eagle will claim an area of several hundred acres, while a robin usually has a territory of roughly an acre.

How does a bird enforce its claim? It may be easy to stake out the territory, but maintaining it is another thing. It is said, "Good fences make good neighbors." But the bird cannot build fences. Birds keep trespassers out of their territory principally by voice. They sing the message—" This land is reserved." Sometimes the birds will strike a threatening posture to protect their area. It is like a man flexing his muscles to indicate he is capable of defending himself. A few birds will even resort to physical force to ward off intruders.

Other members of the wildlife kingdom also stake out their areas. They do this by various ways, often by leaving scent by urination or other markings. The mountain lion in the western United States is somewhat of a loner and is highly territorial. After he stakes out his claim, he resides in the boundaries that he has established. There is a great deal of respect among the lions as to the properties of others. This insures against hunting pressures by other lions in any given area. Males will maintain a range of twenty to one hundred square miles. This will intersect with smaller ranges of several females which average about fifty square miles. The respect for each other's range keeps down the possibility of over-population.

Humans also have built within them a strong desire to have a place of their own. In the places my family have lived we've had a plot of land on which to grow things. Without this piece of land I would feel somewhat detached from the good earth.

Peoples throughout the world all desire a place of their own. Our national songs express this: "God bless our native land; firm may it ever stand," and, "My country 'tis of thee. Sweet land of liberty. Of thee I sing; Land where my fathers died. Land of the pilgrim's pride." Wars have often ensued to protect the land. In the Mid-East today, the struggle between peoples over having land of their own causes much unrest.

Over the centuries, boundaries have been essential to allow people to have a place of their own, and respect for those boundaries is necessary for peace and harmony. God's covenant with Abraham included the land. When Joshua led the Israelites to conquer the promised land, it was divided amongst the twelve tribes so each would have a place of his own. Even when we come to the end of our earthly sojourn and have to relinquish a "place of our own" to someone else, the promise of Jesus is, "I go to prepare a place for you . . . " (John 14:2).

Lord, help us to enjoy a place of our own and to be thankful for it. Also, help us not to be so possessed by our earthly place that we lose sight of our heavenly place.

Being Responsible

Let each one test his own work, and then his reason to boast will be in himself alone and not in his neighbor. For each man will have to bear his own load (Galatians 6:4-5).

If you have ever watched a bird build her nest, you are aware of the tedious task that confronts her. Some nests, like that of the robin, are relatively simple. She uses small sticks and mud with a lining of grass and leaves. However simple the design, the construction involves transporting material, a beak at a time, and then carefully shaping and compacting it. The Baltimore oriole performs an architectural marvel. She suspends her woven nest from a tree branch and it appears like a basket dangling in the wind. I once found such a nest that had a purple thread woven into its intricate design. A pair of bald eagles uses a different procedure. After two young birds mate, the first year will be used in constructing a huge platform nest made out of branches and sticks. The following year they will commence raising a family. Each succeeding year they will add branches to their housing unit.

Building a nest and raising young fledglings is no picnic. It takes a lot of industriousness and energy.

Imagine, then, that some obnoxious bird comes along and is so lazy that it lays its eggs in the nest of birds of another species and leaves the rearing of its young to foster parents. Unbelievable! Yet true. Fortunately, a little less than one percent of all species engage in this activity. The brown-headed cowbird is one of these culprits. The eggs of the cowbird tend to hatch a day or two earlier than those of its typical host, thus giving the cowbird chick a distinct advantage in competing for food from the foster parent. In some cases, the host bird's own chicks will starve for lack of food intake. Robins and blue jays are two birds that have the ability to detect eggs that are not their own and will reject them.

The most skilled bird at escaping homemaking responsibilities is the cuckoo. It scouts out nests in which to lay its eggs, and some cuckoos can lay eggs that match the color of the host's own.

As much as we may dislike this irresponsible behavior among the birds, we must admit that we are often guilty of the same maneuvers. There is an expression that sums it up in the human family: "Let George do it." We want to see a lot of things happen, but we are unwilling to make them happen. We want the schools and the church to straighten out our kids if we have been unable to handle them at home. We want good, clean, and efficient government without having to get involved more than at the ballot box. We've got lots of good ideas on how to improve society, if only someone else will hatch them and develop them. We curse the darkness, but we are hesitant to light a candle and hold it high. For too long we have been willing to lay eggs in someone else's nest, whether it be the government, school, church, or law enforcement; then we sit on the sidelines and hope some big mama will come along and hatch them and raise them.

When World War I ended, Manchester journalist, C. E. Montague, warned his countrymen that reconstruction would happen only if every individual would do his or her job. He said, "To get down to work, whoever else idles; to tell no lies, whoever else may thrive on their use—to take less from your world than you give."

I'm glad that not all birds operate like the cowbird. If they did, there would soon be no birds to watch nor songs to greet the dawn at the breakfast table.

Lord, perhaps I've been sitting in the bleachers too long. Help me get down on the playing field and get in the game of life so I will be a contributor and not only a consumer.

Flowers and Fragrance

For we are the aroma of Christ to God among those that are being saved and among those who are perishing (II Corinthians 2:15).

Tulips have difficulty waiting for the snow to vacate our garden area. They want to thrust up out of the ground and announce that spring has arrived. The other flowers stay in their beds and are not so eager to stretch from their winter nap. Before they heed the wake-up call, the tulips are already blooming with a variety of colors. It is the initial preview of what is to come in the rest of the flower garden. I am grateful for God making the world in technicolor.

The fruit trees do not want to be left behind in the spring parade of color. Our five apple trees begin to bloom profusely. Not only do they become globes of beauty, but the fragrance of their blossoms fill the spring air and beckons us to come and take a closer look. Simultaneously with the apple trees, our grove of wild plum trees, not wanting to be outdone, present us with more viewing pleasure along with their own distinct fragrance.

The old saying is true: April showers bring May flowers. The garden comes alive. Each flower seems to send forth a scent that stirs the memory. When the bushy peony blooms with its large showy flower, the smell brings me back to high school graduation time. For my wife, it brings back the memory from childhood when her youngest brother, Jimmie, at age eleven, was struck down by a car. The room where the casket was placed was filled with bouquets of peonies. To this day the fragrance of peonies rekindles the memory of that event many years ago.

When summer rolls around, our garden becomes a magnetic marvel for insects of the air and hummingbirds that come for a look and a sip of nectar. The various fragrances waft through the air as if a young lady were walking by wearing her favorite alluring perfume.

The rose tops them all. This ancient flower has been cultivated for over 3,000 years. In Roman times, rose petals were strewn ankle deep for the delight of emperors. Today the rose is the flower for saying, "I love you." Its aroma punctuates that statement.

Have you ever thought of yourself as a flower that gives off a fragrance? A few flowers give off a pungent odor that repels. That can also happen with people. An editorial in our paper talked about former President Clinton's immoral behavior during his term of office: "The president made the presidency smell bad. He dishonored his oath of office. He made the nation feel dirty."

But there are many whose lifestyle aroma is attractive, pleasing and upbuilding. Paul talks about this influence to the church at Corinth: "But thanks be to God, who in Christ always leads us in triumph, and through us spreads the fragrance of the knowledge of him everywhere. For we are the aroma of Christ to God among those who are being saved and among those who are perishing, to one a fragrance from death to death, to the other a fragrance of life to life" (II Corinthians 2:14-16).

We make the invisible kingdom visible when the aroma is that of love, peace, service, joy, meekness, forgiveness, compassion, gentleness, self-control; and the list goes on. Love is the rose of the Christian garden. The fragrance of Jesus was vividly described in Carl Sandburg's *To a Contemporary Bunkshooter:* "Jesus had a way of talking soft and, outside a few bankers and higher-ups among the con men of Jerusalem, everybody liked to have this Jesus around because he never made any fake passes and everything he said went and he helped the sick and gave people hope. This Jesus was good to look at, smelled good, listened good. He threw out something fresh and beautiful from the skin of his body and the touch of his hands wherever he passed along" (Chicago Poems).

Dear Lord, may my Christian lifestyle be attractive so others will be drawn to you. Forgive me when my behavior has been more like a repellant than a contagion.

Pain Becomes Gain

More than that, we rejoice in our sufferings, knowing that suffering produces endurance, and endurance produces character, and character produces hope, and hope does not disappoint us, because God's love has been poured into our hearts through the Holy Spirit that has been given us (Romans 5:3-5).

One early spring evening, ominous clouds were rolling into the Rocky Mountain area. As they hovered overhead, the lightning lit up the dark sky, followed by ear-splitting cracks of thunder. One large bolt of electrical power crashed into a very tall pine tree, which was standing on sentinel duty on top of a high crest in the mountains. The tree trunk was split as if a mighty axe came bearing down on it. Then fire broke out, and it was the beginning of the end for many acres of magnificent forest.

All life was seemingly destroyed as the forest became a charred battlefield. The trees that were left standing appeared as blackened telephone poles. But in this desolate scene there sprang a new promise of life. The lodge pole pine had previously sprinkled the ground with its hard shell seeds. These seeds can remain in the ground for twenty to thirty years until a fire cracks open the hard pods and releases the seeds. Within a few years, new life and a new forest is under construction. Adversity brings the advent of a new beginning.

Nature provides us with another example of pain becoming gain. The mollusk called an oyster gets an alien grain of sand caught within its shell. This intruder imposes pain and distress, like a grain of sand in your shoe. However, the oyster cannot extricate it and so learns to live with this annoying grain of sand. It begins to secrete a milky-like organic substance around the grain of sand. Many layers of this substance, which is a material similar to the interior of the mollusk, gradually make a pearl. A piece of pain has been transformed into a thing of wondrous beauty and delight.

The cross of Calvary is the monumental symbol of how our Lord took the pain of human sin on himself and made that cross an instrument of redemptive power. He teaches us that through the power of his Spirit we can turn our adversity into life, our pain into joy, our sorrows into new growth.

Suffering in and of itself is incapable of altering life for the better. Cancer, heart trouble, and accidents are morally neutral. They are powerless to make either saints or cynics, wise or foolish. Milk, butter, eggs, and flour have no power to make a cake unless the creative mind uses these ingredients in the proper process. Without that, they will turn rancid and useless. Suffering and sorrow, unless used by the creative mind, can swerve a soul into sourness. But mixed with God's grace, sorrow may produce the cake of character.

The Arabs have a saying that all sunshine and no rain makes a desert. Without the tears of sorrow and adversity, the soil of the soul might dry up. Karl Barth noted, "The generation that has no great anguish on its heart will have no great music on its lips." Much great art and music has been spawned in the beds of sorrow. In our adversities we find an opportunity to understand others and to serve others who are hurting. Rather than denying, running away, or blaming others for our pains, by God's help we can turn them into something beneficial.

Henri Matisse (1869-1954) was a great French painter. Toward the end of his life, he suffered from a crippling form of arthritis that deformed his hands, making it agonizing for him to even hold the brush. He placed bits of cloth between his fingers to keep the brush from slipping. One day, an apprentice who was distressed by watching the old man labor under such pain said, "Why do you go on like this, sir? Why continue to paint when it causes so much misery?" The old artist smiled and replied, "The pain passes, but the beauty remains."

Lord of the cross, forgive me for trying to avoid all difficulties and obstacles. Help me to believe that you will give me strength to cope with any task or adversity which life places in front of me.

Respecting Privacy

Love one another with brotherly affection; outdo one another in showing honor (Romans 12:10).

The beautiful old brick church is located on the on shore of a small lake near Dresser, Wisconsin. Next to the church is the parsonage that one of our sons and his family call home. Huge white pine trees, some of which are over one hundred years old, populate the spacious yard. A year ago, a pair of bald eagles staked claim to one of the stately pines. They started a building project, without a permit, near the top of the tree. Sticks and branches of various sizes were the basic building materials. The pair of eagles seemed to be in no hurry to finish the task as they took some long breaks to go fishing. They were not planning to start a family until next spring, so all summer and fall they leisurely went about their carpentry.

While visiting our son, I watched these two majestic birds come flying onto their newly constructed home. They were images of gracefulness and power. They seemed to fly effortlessly. In a power dive, eagles have been clocked at 120 miles per hour. These birds have great affection for each other and mate for life.

Our son has spent many hours studying the habits of these magnificent birds. He related one unusual trait that he has noted on several occasions. While working in his garden, not very far from the base of the tree which the eagles chose as home, the birds did not seem to mind his presence. However, as soon as he stopped and looked up at the nest, the eagle would fly off, vacating the area. He also observed that when Sunday school children would come over from church to look and point at the nest, the eagles would leave.

It seemed as though the eagle would tolerate someone in the vicinity as long as that person did not invade its privacy by staring and pointing. That would make the eagle uncomfortable and nervous.

We are not unlike the bald eagles in my son's backyard. If folks stare at us or give us undue attention it causes a disturbing feeling. We have lost our "space." The "paparazzi" that run with their cameras to get close-up pictures of celebrities are perhaps at the top of the list of those who invade another person's privacy. We are now also becoming concerned about the Internet computer world which seems to become ever closer at peeking into the private world of individuals. It is interesting to note that the Scriptures picture Jesus as one who knocks at the door of the individual, hoping to be invited in. He could just break down the door and enter, but he respects our choice of accepting or rejecting.

"Behold, I stand at the door and knock; if anyone hears my voice and opens the door, I will come in to him and eat with him, and he with me" (Revelation 3:20).

It all boils down to the matter of kindness, courtesy, and respect. Ralph Waldo Emerson said, "Life is not so short but there is always time for courtesy." We do not hear very many sermons about good manners or the practicing of courtesy. But for the Christian, gentlemanly and ladylike behavior is still in vogue. Oliver Wendell Holmes said, "Good breeding is surface Christianity."

Paul states that love is "kind . . . not arrogant or rude" (I Corinthians 13:4-5). Where there is such Christian love, honor is safe, and personality is sacred and respected. Once, a guest at a dinner given in honor of Marshal Foch was behaving rather rudely and as a matter of rationalization said to the marshal, "There is nothing but so much air in French politeness." Quietly the marshal retorted, "Neither is there anything but air in a pneumatic tire, and yet it wonderfully eases the jolts along life's highway."

Lord, forgive me for prying into another person's life without being invited. Help me not to suffocate my friends by being too close.

Listen and Follow

Listen to me, my people, and give ear to me, my nation; for a law will go forth from me, and my justice for a light to the peoples (Isaiah 51:4).

Nature was yawning and stretching. It was time to wake up from the winter nap. The tulips and daffodils were sticking their necks out to check the weather. The birds seemed to be loosening up their vocal cords for some spring concerts. I eagerly awaited the arrival of my favorite duck—the wood duck. The wood duck is one of North America's most brilliantly colored waterfowl. Each spring, several wood ducks make our pond, which is nestled in a woods of elm, maple, and oak trees, their home. Some of the older trees have hollow cavities created by woodpeckers, squirrels or decay. These holes are custom-made homes, ready for occupancy.

The day arrived when, tumbling out of the sky like maple leaves, the wood ducks were back from the south to set up the new house-keeping season. The male ducks would hang around long enough for their mates to find adequate housing in which to raise a family, and then they would take off for regions unknown to me. Evidently the males felt no parental responsibilities.

The average height of a wood duck home is ten to twenty feet above the ground. However, I once saw a wood duck flying into a cavity which was close to forty feet high and located a considerable distance from a body of water. When the nesting site has been selected, the female begins to pluck down feathers from her breast, forming a soft insulated area for as many as six to a dozen eggs. She does not start incubating until the last egg is laid. This ensures that all the eggs will hatch at approximately the same time.

When the ducklings hatch, they do not linger for days or weeks in the nest. They are not fed in the nest. Therefore, the ducklings usually leave the nest within twenty-four hours. Of course, they cannot fly when they abandon the place of their birth.

Since they are hatched in a cavity, how do they get out to the world awaiting them? They cannot be pushed out. They must be encouraged to climb out of the hole and then plummet to the earth beneath the nest. This is where a miracle of nature enters into the drama. Two or three days before the ducklings break out of their shells, the mother duck does an amazing thing. She listens for the faint peeping inside the eggs, and then she communicates back to them. This ritual familiarizes the duckling to the sound of her voice even before they hatch. Experiments have been conducted which reveal that communication in this manner is crucial for the ducklings. Without it they might not respond as quickly to her commands and coaxing.

The day to leave the nest arrives. The mother wood duck flutters to the ground and then looks up to the small opening many feet above her. She gives the signal, and one by one the ducklings scramble up to the opening. Even though they cannot fly, they jump at the mother's command. If the nest were twenty feet high it would be equivalent of a man jumping two hundred feet. If a duckling were unwilling to jump, death by starvation would come in the nest. When the brood are out of the nest and reach the water, there are enemies such as turtles, snakes, hawks, and raccoons. Only by staying close to their mother and listening to her commands will they have the hope of survival.

Jesus said, "My sheep hear my voice, and I know them, and they follow me; and I will give them eternal life, and they will never perish, and no one shall snatch them out of my hand" (John 10:27).

We need to listen to His voice!
Trust and obey, there is no other way,
To be happy in Jesus; but to trust and obey.

Lord, I confess that obedience does not come easily. Your commands have sometimes gone unheeded. Help me to see that obedience to you brings joy and life and that my obedience to you demonstrates my love to you.

Changing Clothes

*Put off your old nature, which belongs to your former manner of life
... and put on the new nature, created after the likeness of God in true
righteousness and holiness (Ephesians 4:22-24).*

How often have you looked at your wardrobe wistfully thinking
of getting something new? Some people wear clothes until they become threadbare; others are captivated by new styles and fabrics and
are on a continual shopping spree for new apparel. There are folks
who hang unto old clothes as if they are keepsakes, while others either
have garage sales or take trips to thrift stores with unwanted clothing.
There are clothes which are easily repairable, and also those that seem
to defy mending.

However you manage your dressing habits, there is usually a
good feeling when you experience a new change of apparel.

Did you know that birds need a complete change of clothes?
Feathers cannot be repaired, so from time to time, after considerable
wear and tear, the bird goes through a molting period in order to
acquire a new wardrobe. During the molting, worn feathers loosen in
their sockets and are pushed out by new feathers growing behind
them.

Young birds go through several molting periods before receiving adult plumage. Once an adult, the molting generally takes place at
a certain time each year. It is usually timed not to overlap with periods
of breeding or migration. Songbirds frequently molt in late summer.
They do not lose all their flight feathers at once, for that would cause
them to be grounded and helpless.

Some birds, like the ptarmigan, change feathers twice a year.
Winter plumage often includes more feathers for increased insulation.

Ptarmigans molt for camouflage purposes, switching from their brown summer feathers to an all-white look for winter in the Arctic regions.

The molting process varies in the amount of time it takes from one species to another. Some make the change in less than a month, while others take a longer time to change, from one to three months.

Ducks and geese take a different course of action in their wardrobe change. They lose all their flight feathers at once and replace them in a couple weeks. Thus, they are flightless for a short period of time and attempt to hide out in secluded lakes and ponds where they feel safe from predators.

My mind takes me on a journey o'er the days of my life. I am something like the bird that needs to continually shed the old and put on the new. Theologically, we call it sanctification. It is the lifelong process of the Christian growing in faith and Christ-likeness all the days of his or her life. Some grow more quickly than others, just like some birds go through a feather change more rapidly than some of their other feathered friends. But if you are to grow through the work of God's Spirit within you, there must be a willing change.

A man was once asked what it felt like to be a Christian on the inside. He mused a bit and then said, "Well, it's like I've got two dogs inside me. One is a good dog, and the other a bad dog, and they are always fighting." His questioner asked, "Which dog is winning?" The quick answer came, "Whichever one I feed." So it is with the growth of our spiritual lives.

"Therefore, my beloved, as you have always obeyed, so now, not only as in my presence but much more in my absence, work out your own salvation with fear and trembling; for God is at work in you, both to will and to work for his good pleasure" (Philippians 2:12-13).

Lord, teach me the lesson of the molting process. I get stuck in a rut and seem adverse to Change in my life. May I grow some new flight feathers, so I can soar higher.

Pretending

But by the grace of God I am what I am (I Corinthians 15:10).

One summer, a killdeer decided to set up housekeeping on the side of our rather long gravel driveway. To me, it seemed like a very inappropriate place, for there was little vegetation to camouflage the nest. But, of course, I did not understand the ways of the killdeer. The nest was merely a slight depression lined with pebbles. Prior to the nesting time, I would see the killdeer darting across our meadow, stopping as suddenly as it started to inspect the ground for insects and bugs.

However, when the eggs were being laid and the hatching began, the killdeer performed a maneuver which was very fascinating. When a person or my dog came close to the nest the killdeer displayed its dramatic "broken wing" act. Dragging its wing along the ground as if injured, it would distract predators away from its eggs or young. The killdeer is a great pretender.

Another of the animal kingdom that has developed the art of pretending is the opossum. It habitually feigns death when frightened. Thus, its predator might amble on thinking there is only a wrapped up bundle of fur. From this antic we have developed the phrase "playing opossum."

As animals pretend in order to protect themselves, we seem to do likewise. We wear masks so that people will not know exactly what we are. For that reason, we oftentimes pretend to be what we really are not.

Freud, Jung, and Adler, three leading psychologists, had different views on our greatest need. Freud said man's greatest need was to be loved. Jung said it was security, while Adler said the greatest need was significance.

It is quite revealing that in pursuit of these things we most frequently put on the mask of pretense.

Think back on your courtship years. A young fellow meets a beautiful young woman that he really wants. In order to win her, he puts his best foot forward and endeavors to be the kind of person he feels she will respond to. He thus pretends to be something that he really isn't at all. If she is attracted to him, chances are she, too, will show her best side so she will get the ring on her finger. After they are married, the masks of pretending come off, and each sees a stranger emerging from the person they thought they knew.

But we seem to keep on pretending to protect or promote ourselves: sometimes to hide inferiority feelings, sometimes to cover a lie, sometimes to impress someone, sometimes to escape reality. All this deception ultimately becomes a deadly game as the masks eventually seem to come off.

The only real cure for the pretending game is the unconditional love of God. He accepts me, warts and all. I no longer need to pretend to be something I am not. I can face both my vices and my virtues and by the grace and mercy of God set about to see his Spirit change my vices.

Freedom comes only when we set aside our masks and stop the game of pretending.

The apostle Paul, in his writings, bared his soul and allowed us to see him as he really was. Making no apologies, he says, "But by the grace of God I am what I am" (I Corinthians 15:10).

Nathaniel Hawthorne once said, "No man can for any considerable time, wear one face to himself, and another to the multitude, without finally getting bewildered as to which one is the true one."

Pretending is a precarious game! It is living a lie.

Lord, I need to be reassured that you accept me just as I am. Help me realize it is your love that enables me to accept myself and begin to make positive changes. May all my pretending become a thing of the past.

The Joy of Living

My heart and flesh sing for joy to the living God (Psalm 84:2).

The river otter lives near swift mountain streams, rivers, and marshes. It gives birth from one to six pups which are blind and helpless at birth. At somewhere between six and nine weeks, otter pups take their first swim in the company of their mothers. The otter will grow to an average weight of thirty pounds and is active at all times of the day and night. It is the only member of the weasel family with a webbed foot and can swim up to seven miles an hour. The river otter eats many other smaller animals, such as snails, turtles, crabs, and snakes. Fish is its favorite food, and it will eat it as we would a hot dog, from one end to the other. It is able to pierce the skin of the fish and crush the bones with sharp, strong teeth.

Both parents share the responsibility of raising the young. They are openly affectionate and loyal. In fact, they have been known to mourn, even wail, for days when a mate or family member is lost or killed. It has been witnessed that an otter might remain by the lifeless body of a mate for days without food.

One of the most interesting characteristics of the otter is that they are famous for their exuberance at play. Siblings romp with each other for hours, slipping in and out of the water and using muddy riverbanks as slides. They perform belly flops and rollovers, and love to play tag. They turn the mundane job of survival into fun. Although catching food is a serious matter for most wildlife, to the otter, it is often play time. Frequently the otter is more interested in the sport of the chase than securing a meal. It might play with the fish and then release it.

Irenaeus once said, "A man fully alive is the glory of God." The early Christian writer Tertullian said, "The Christian saint is hilarious." Those expressions convey the idea that the Christian ought to have the playful joy of the otter. But in reality, it is often not the case. In May, 1659, a law was passed by the Massachusetts Bay Colony: "Whoever shall be found observing any such day as Christmas or the like, either by forbearing labor, feasting, or any other way, as a festival, shall be fined five shillings." Needless to say, the colonists had not found the Jesus of joy. Religion had become an oppressive cloud of doom and seriousness.

There is a story of the taxicab driver who declared that when a group of people came to a church convention in his city, they came with the Ten Commandments in one hand and a ten-dollar bill in the other, and they never broke either one. Certainly the Christian lives under moral obligations, but to the world we are often considered as somber, long-faced individuals that have lost much of the joy of life.

At Pentecost, the Christians were so hilarious that the people said they must be drunk. The early followers of St. Francis of Assisi had this gaiety. They were so happy, they had to be reproved for laughing in church. Seventy times in the New Testament the Christian is called upon to rejoice and be full of joy; we are assured that when God's Spirit is in us we will be filled with joy, for the "fruit of the Spirit is joy."

Jesus was a popular dinner guest. His enemies called him a glutton and a winebibber. He merely did not conform to their dusty code of conduct. Now, we know that a sad man with no humor and love of life is never a popular dinner guest. And we know that children do not flock to a man who knows not how to smile and laugh. We, like the otter, need to learn the joy of play, so our Christian witness becomes appealing and contagious.

Lord, help me to not take myself too seriously. Enable me to laugh at myself. May I laugh with others and not at them. May I see the need for play time when good fun is the order of the day.

Planting Trees

I planted. Appolos watered, but God gave the growth (I Corinthians 3:6).

As you drive through the plains of North and South Dakota, you will notice long lines of trees called shelter belts. Farmers have planted these rows of trees and shrubs for the purpose of curbing the effects of the wind, which scrapes off the precious topsoil and sends it sailing through the sky to other regions. During the drought of the 1930s, there was a dust bowl in the plains area, and great amounts of dirt were lost. Consequently, fast-growing trees were planted to conserve the land for farming. An additional bonus was that the shelter belts would stop blowing snow in the winter season and thus preserve moisture for the fields. Wildlife also appreciated these plantings, for they provided nesting and hiding habitat.

In mountainous and hilly country, trees keep soil from washing down the steep banks. The root systems of the trees and shrubs hold the precious soil in place, halting erosion. An example of the tremendous loss caused by erosion is the estimated 730 million tons of silt deposited each year in the Gulf of Mexico by the Mississippi River. This great amount of sediment is picked up along the long course of the river. More trees and better conservation practices would alleviate much of the loss of the important resource of soil.

The long shelter belts of the plains region remind me of an important truth about the Christian life. The business of planting trees of goodness and righteousness should occupy more of my time than of going hunting for the manifestations of evil. Positive, affirming action is more necessary than negative haranguing. The Quakers have a motto: "It is better to light a candle than to curse the darkness." That is solid advice. Yet it sometimes seems easier to get people to march in a crusade against something than to get them to stand for something.

Tree planting is proactive and is certainly a preventative measure. Jesus tells the story of the wheat and the weeds (Matthew 13:24 ff). He is saying that human judgment is too limited to uproot all evil without also destroying much that is good. The weeds in the parable were probably darnel, which looks very much like wheat when young, but later can be distinguished. We are instructed to concentrate on cultivating the good wheat and leaving the elimination of the weeds to the judgment of God. Historically, we know that many efforts to uproot evil have not contributed to the creation of what is good. It has sometimes led to fanaticism, which has created more evil in its wake. The Crusades serve as an example of this.

Of course, in our Christian moral concern, we must take a stand against forms of evil, but in so doing realize that in a broken world there will never be total eradication of the poison of evil. More time and energy should be spent promoting the positive aspects of the Christian faith. Scripture says, "Do not be overcome by evil but overcome evil with good" (Romans 12:21). An old pastor once told me, "The best way to fight Satan is to serve the Lord."

If you have adjacent rooms connected by a doorway, you may want to try this experiment. Some night, turn on a bright light in one room. Close the door to the adjacent room, which now is in total darkness. Now open the door. Does the darkness sneak into the lighted room? Not at all. The light travels into the dark room and the lighted room remains as bright as before. Such is the penetrating power of light. The Gospel, too, has this power as we live out our Christian faith in the world. It permeates the darkened world and brings hope to the human condition. The best way to stop erosion of the precious soil of the soul is to plant trees of faith, hope, and love in our minds, family, neighborhood, and world.

Dear Jesus, it is said of you that you "went about doing good" (Acts 10:38). Help me to spend more time and energy accentuating the positive virtues and activities of life rather than always concentrating on that which is negative.

The Importance of Mountains

I will lift up my eyes to the hills. From whence does my help come? My help comes from the Lord, who made heaven and earth (Psalm 121:1-2).

I was at the seminary wondering what I should do during the summer break. A friend and I decided to buy an old car and head west. Neither of us had ever visited that part of our country, so off we went. As we approached the Rocky Mountain range, it appeared they were only a few miles down the road. How mistaken we were! The hugeness of the snow-covered peaks was deceiving. That which seemed close was far off in the distance. Finally arriving at the foot of the mountain range, we stopped the car and just stared at the summit. We were awestruck. Ever since then, mountains have mesmerized me.

Mountaintops are not to live on, but to visit for new perspectives and fresh insights. Mountains are symbols of quests that challenge us to reach out with every fiber of our bodies and souls for the fullness of life. They thrust upward as if God were calling the human spirit to soar in the sky of his grace.

I suppose most of us have to confess that we frequently set our sights on easily attainable goals rather than those which will stretch our energies and expand our abilities. Frank Lloyd Wright was an exceptionally good architect. Perhaps, though, he was not always right on his philosophy of life. He once said that public rooms should only be about twelve feet high so people in them would not have to feel insignificant or inferior. The late columnist Dorothy Thompson read that and replied, "The G.I. Joes whom I saw standing awestruck in the Salisbury Cathedral, or watching the robed procession climb the vast stairs of Canterbury, or kneeling under the lofty arches of Notre Dame, or staring upward in St. Peter's at Michelangelo's immense dome, were not feeling insignificant. On the contrary, they were realizing that life has a grandeur and a beauty and a significance above and beyond themselves that wakened in them high aspiration." I would say, "Amen" to that.

It is one of the heresies of our time to bring things down to our lower levels. Books contain the language of the street. Movies and television often show us at our worst and not at our best. Music, in the ears of many of us oldsters, has frequently been reduced to more noise than harmony. People often lift their gaze no higher than their navels.

The height to which a person grows is commensurate with the person's vision. Set your ceiling at only twelve feet, and eventually you will be living underground. The Bible is packed with stories of little people looking up: people who like us, saw a great thing and then became what they saw. Transformation took place and there was a dramatic change in their lives. It was true of Isaiah. He was in the temple, and he "saw the Lord seated on a throne, high and exalted" (Isaiah 6:1). That day he volunteered to be a prophet to his people. Lured by that loftiness in the temple, he was lifted up to a great calling. The boy in Nathaniel Hawthorne's "The Great Stone Face" spent hours and days gazing at the face on the mountain, and slowly he began to bear the image in himself of the face he had looked upon so long.

Worship calls us to look up, as the psalmist did, to the hills. Our faith encourages us to look up into the glory of Christ who puts no ceilings over human life. He knows our potential, and he wants to unlock it.

Lord, I must confess that I have been too complacent and content to live with things as they are, rather than with a vision of what they could be. Help me to set my mind on things above, so my life will stretch and grow.

Those That Wait

But they that wait for the Lord shall renew their strength . . . (Isaiah 40:41).

Occasionally, I have watched a large snapping turtle slowly amble across our lawn heading toward our small pond. He never seems to be in a rush to reach his destination. Time is not a factor in his journey. He doesn't mind if you walk over and observe him at close range. However, if you take a stick and poke him in the face, he will show you he can live up to his name, snapper. He belongs to that group of animals called reptiles.

In general, reptiles play a waiting game. While many birds and mammals hurry and scurry, most reptiles prefer to lie around and let the world come to them. Since they do not rely on metabolic processes to heat their bodies, their caloric requirements are lower than warm-blooded animals. Consequently, their food intake is much less. A rattlesnake in North America would consume only three times its body weight in a year, while a little mole, constantly digging around in the ground, will eat three times its body weight in prey every week. The shrew, one of the smallest mammals, has such rapid metabolism that it eats twice its weight in a twenty-four hour period.

Since most reptiles are not constantly foraging around for food, they lead a somewhat sedentary life. A fifty-year-old snapping turtle may lie at the bottom of a shallow pond for several weeks in the same spot, moving only its neck to strike at a passing fish or frog. He may spend the entire winter without breathing at the bottom of an ice-covered swamp.

Reptiles depend entirely on external heat to keep their bodies in their ideal temperature range. Therefore, you will see them frequently basking on rocks and soil warmed by the sun. The warm temperatures start their engines, enabling them to move more efficiently.

How unlike the reptiles are we humans. We seem to measure life only by activity and productivity. Progress seems to dictate that life must give us more and more of everything faster and faster. There are more cars traveling more roads. There are more televisions with more programs. Computers are quickly outdated with newer ones spitting out more information more and more quickly. And we get caught up on the roller coaster, not knowing where the end of the ride really is.

Waiting, in this fast-paced world, becomes a dirty word. Yet we are exhorted by the Sacred Writings: "Be still before the Lord, wait patiently for him" (Psalm 37:7). And again, "I waited for the Lord; he inclined to me and heard my cry" (Psalm 40:1). It is erroneous to always measure life by some external gauge of productivity. In quietness and stillness there is maybe the best potential for growth in matters that really count.

My father was an example of one who learned the art of purposeful waiting. At age fifty he had to deal with Parkinson's disease. An active life quickly came to a halt, and he was confined to bed. For close to twenty years, he was an invalid. The world perhaps thought his productivity had ended. However, the power of his prayer life will only be measured by eternity's standards.

John Milton (1608-1674) went totally blind at age 44. He wrestled with the question as to whether God exacted labor when light is denied. Could he still serve? The second stanza of "On His Blindness" goes like this:

I fondly ask; but patience, to prevent
That murmur, soon replies, God doth not need
Either man's work or his own gifts, who
Bear his mild yoke, they serve him best, his state
Is Kingly. Thousands at his bidding speed,
And post o'er Land and Ocean without rest:
They also serve who only stand and wait.

Lord, we know that there are some things for which we must work and others for which we must wait. Give us wisdom to know the difference.

One Dies—Another Lives

If by the Spirit you put to death the deeds of the body you will live (Romans 8:13).

It was at Eagle Lake in Ontario, Canada, where we were fishing walleyes. There are countless miles of irregular shoreline on this huge body of water, which is sprinkled with rocky islands. I looked up and spotted a magnificent bald eagle silhouetted against the blue sky, sailing effortlessly as it searched for food. It, too, was fishing. Scanning the water with its acute vision, it evidently spotted a fish near the water's surface. The wings were half folded as it dove decisively for the fish. Plummeting toward the water, it quickly came out of its dive with spread wings, and with a swift precise motion, talons outstretched, it grabbed the fish. On powerful wings, it soared to the branch of a tall, dead white pine and began to tear into the flesh of the fish with its sharp beak. One living creature died that another could live.

A red fox walked slowly across a snow-covered field. He listened for the slightest movement of a mouse in the grass beneath the snow. When his keen ears pinpointed the location of the sound, the fox leaped into the air and pounced on the mouse. The mouse was a tasty morsel for the red fox. Again, one living creature died that another could live.

In my adventures in the great outdoors, I've seen many incidents of one creature living by the death of another. Once I observed a great horned owl capture a muskrat and with great difficulty become airborne with the weight of his catch. The muskrat squealed, as it became a victim of this bird of prey.

Nature certainly seems violent. Life and death are daily occurrences in the law of the field. A cougar stalks a deer. A rabbit's pain becomes a golden eagle's gain. A snake swallows a frog whole. Each survives by another's demise.

This principle that nothing lives unless something else dies is found not only in the world of nature, but also in the jungle of the human heart. The sinful inclinations of the flesh must fall victim to the influence of the Holy Spirit. That is why Paul says, "Put to death therefore what is earthly in you: fornication, impurity, passion, evil desire, and covetousness, which is idolatry" (Colossians 3:5). It will lead to depression of the spirit if you attempt to be committed to Christ and the world at the same time.

Hatred must die *so* love may live.
Resentment must die so forgiveness may live.
Despair must die so hope may live.
Pride must die so humility may live.
Cruelty must die so sensitivity may live.

The list could go on and on. Just as the animals of prey must continue their violent ways in order to live, we also must continue to put to death those things which separate us from God and one another if we are to live spirit-filled lives. Martin Luther says it well in his catechism concerning the daily meaning of baptism: "It means that our sinful self, with all its evil deeds and desires, should be drowned through daily repentance; and that day after day a new self should arise to live with God in righteousness and purity forever."

Lord, I confess that I have not always wrestled successfully against the sinful desires within me. Help me to "throw off everything that hinders and the sin that easily entangles" that I may run with perseverance that race you have marked out for me.

Equipped For The Task

Now may the God of peace who brought again from the dead our Lord Jesus, the great shepherd of the sheep, by the blood of the eternal covenant, equip you with everything good that you may do his will, working in you that which is pleasing in his sight, through Jesus Christ; to whom be glory for ever and ever. Amen (Hebrews 13:20-21).

While living in Wisconsin, we had a farm acreage cradled in the hill country not far from the Mississippi River. A trout stream meandered through the valley with tree-covered hills standing guard over the farmstead. At night it became a scary, haunted place for our small children. The shadows created by the high hills formed ghostly apparitions. The whippoorwill sang its eerie song. The bats fluttered through the evening sky seeking flying insects. The frogs croaked with discordant sounds. Added to all this, there was frequently the hooting of a great horned owl, known as the "tiger of the air." To me, the sounds of the night were exciting; to our children, they were frightening.

One summer when I was raising some wild mallard ducks, one of them disappeared every evening. I thought maybe a raccoon or fox was paying me a visit, but there were no tracks to be seen. I set a trap with a dead pigeon as bait. The next morning the thief was caught—a great horned owl.

The great horned owl is also known as a hoot owl and ranges in size from eighteen to twenty-five inches. The female is slightly larger than the male. The bird is equipped in a special way for its tasks. Many of the rodents the owl hunts are more active at night, so the owl needs special vision. The owl has more rod cells in its retina than most birds do. These gather whatever light is available, allowing it to "see in the dark." Its iris expands and contracts quickly. Due to the placement of the eyes, the great horned owl has binocular vision– that is, an overlapping of each eye's field of vision, giving it greater ability to judge distance. Another feature of the eye is a third eyelid that cleanses and moisturizes the eyes like a windshield washer and wiper.

The second thing that equips the owl for hunting is its amazing hearing. The feathery tufts on the head of the owl, which give the bird its name, are not ears at all. The real ears are precisely positioned in different locations on each side of the head. This results in sound reaching each ear at a different instant, enabling the owl to accurately pinpoint the exact source of a squeaking mouse.

The third great asset that equips the owl is the intricate feather structure in the wings. The wing feathers have frayed edges. As the air passes over the feathers it is broken up, and the sound level of the flapping is reduced to almost nothing. This enables the owl to approach its prey swiftly and silently. Contrast this to the sound of a low-flying flock of ducks going overhead on a still autumn morning. You can easily hear the wings beating the air.

If God, in his creative powers, so equipped the owl for the tasks it must perform, will he not also equip us for the tasks he calls us to do? I believe so! Abraham, Moses, David, Amos, Paul, and God's saints of all ages were given special gifts to perform ministries which they were ordained to do. God does not send us forth empty-handed into the vineyards of life. The unique tools each one needs are provided. He does not always provide what we want, but always provides what we need. Paul writes about the various gifts or manifestations God gives: "To each is given the manifestation of the Spirit for the common good" (I Corinthians 12:7). He also declares that we are equipped for the Christian life through the Scriptures: "All scripture is inspired by God and profitable for teaching, for reproof, for correction, for training in righteousness, that the man of God may be complete, equipped for every good work" (II Timothy 3:16).

Dear Lord, you provide us with the proper equipment to accomplish the tasks you set before us. Help us to believe that you never send us into battle without necessary supplies.

Osmosis

*And that Christ may dwell in your hearts through faith; that you,
being rooted and grounded in love . . . (Ephesians 3:17).*

My father loved to plant trees, and he spent many hours caring
for them. This love relationship with trees was passed on to me. Stately
trees must also have intrigued the psalmist as he described the godly
man as "a tree planted by streams of water that yields fruit in its season" (Psalm 1:3).

In order to grow, trees need an adequate supply of water. When
I was a small boy, I wondered how they could drink water from the
soil. I was puzzled. Over the years, I learned about root structure and
the process of osmosis.

Roots not only anchor the tree, but also are the collectors of
water. Many trees have a central tap root which reaches deep into the
soil, giving the tree great stability. Also, there are a series of branch
roots that reach out in all directions. On the roots there are tiny cellu-
lar projections that may be only one-third of an inch in length. These
are called root hairs. Their myriad number enables them to absorb
enormous quantities of water. The passage of water and dissolved min-
erals through a semi-permeable membrane in the root hairs is called
osmosis. This process is a gradual and subtle pressure.

When Paul prays that the Ephesian church would be rooted and
grounded in love, he knew what he was talking about. He wanted
them to experience the security and nourishment that comes from
having their roots deeply planted in Christ's love.

This phenomenon of osmosis has some remarkable parallels to
life. The environments in which we grow influence us all. That influence may be positive or negative and is often imperceptible at its be-
ginnings.

I knew a college student from Chicago who had little church interest. He was a good student and an outstanding athlete but had no concern for Christianity. After hearing "repent, repent" many times, he became hostile, shutting himself off completely, and refused to even consider the Christian message as anything but a fairy tale. But in the environment of a Christian college, something was happening. This is what he wrote:

> "Here I was, walking in the middle of a Christian environment, and yet completely shut off from it. It was like a lifeboat scene where people die of thirst though surrounded by an ocean of water. But you can't spend four years at a Christian college without some change taking place. And that's about what happened. I picked up the skeleton outline of facts which go with the Christian message—through osmosis, that is."

That is when his story began to change. Through the work of the Holy Spirit, he began to see Jesus and himself in a different light and soon committed himself to the Lord. After a short stint as a professional football player, he became a missionary, a college president, a professor, and a pastor.

Perhaps the process of osmosis also played a part in the change of Peter and John, who spent much time in the presence of Jesus. Luke says, "Now when they saw the boldness of Peter and John, and perceived that they were uneducated, common men, they wondered; and they recognized that they had been with Jesus" (Act 4:13).

Negatively, one wonders what osmosis might play in the lives of the average American child when you consider that when a child reaches mid-adolescence, he has watched 15,000 hours of television. That is more time that he spends with teachers, friends, or parents. Add to this other forms of media, and we have to agree the influence is great.

W. Clement Stone wrote:" Be careful the environment you choose for it will shape you; be careful the friends you choose for you will become like them."

Lord, give me the wisdom to spend time in places and with persons that will build me up and not tear me down. Help me to be a good influence in the lives of others.

Good Communication

This is the message we have heard from him and proclaim to you,
that God is light and in him is no darkness at all (I John 1:5).

We have a large flower and vegetable garden in our back yard and two flower gardens in the front of the house. When the blooms began to appear, the honeybees move in to collect nectar. The phrase "busy as a bee" was coined from watching these little honey-makers go about their work. If the plants could talk, they would express their gratitude for all the pollination that happens because of the bees' activity.

The honeybee colony consists of three castes: the queen bee, many thousand workers (sexually undeveloped females), and a few hundred drones (fertile males). The workers bear the burden of maintaining the hive, caring for the larva, and gathering and preparing the nectar. The workers live for only about six weeks during the active season. Those that hatch in the fall live through the winter. The drones die in the fall.

One of the miracles of the honeybee is found in the bee's ability to communicate accurately to each other. The scout or forager bee returns to the hive and relates the distance of the nectar source by its body motion. If the bee performs a circular motion, it indicates the nectar supply is within a hundred yards. A figure eight reveals the nectar is over one hundred yards away. The tail-wagging of the bee is in direct proportion to the distance: the closer the source, the more intense body motion.

The bee then uses the sun as a reference point. If the bee points its body vertically on the comb of the hive, it signals that the flowers are located away from the hive in the same direction as the sun.

A downward position indicates the flowers are in the opposite direction. Even the bee's angle on the comb gives a distinct message.

Directions are crucial, because the worker bee carries only enough fuel with which to reach its destination. If a bee carries too little, the bee will fall and die before the flower area is reached unless another source of glucose is found along the way.

The honeybee provides us with an amazing lesson on the need for cooperation and the necessity of reliable communication.

In 490 B. C., the Greek army under Miltiades defeated a large Persian army at Marathon, over twenty miles from Athens. It was one of the decisive battles of history, for the whole existence of the state of Athens was at stake. A runner, Pheidipidies, ran all the way to Athens carrying the news. He gasped out one word, "Victory," and then dropped dead.

This historical event was portrayed in a cartoon that depicted a runner with a torch coming swiftly to a crowd of anxious Athenians and the caption read, "I forgot the message." What a letdown! The messenger forgot words that could carry matters of life and death.

It is of salient significance that the church of all ages needs to communicate the message clearly. It is a matter of life and death! Paul said, "Woe to me if I do not preach the Gospel" (I Corinthians 9:16). Again, "For I delivered to you as of first importance what I also received, that Christ died for our sins in accordance with the Scriptures, that he was buried, that he was raised on the third day in accordance with the Scriptures" (I Corinthians 15:3-4). When talking about prophecy and tongues, Paul warns against words without meaning. He said, "And if the bugle gives an indistinct sound, who will get ready for battle?" I Corinthians 14:8). The bee says, "Beware of giving mixed messages."

Lord, I need to realize that others cannot read my mind. Help me to be more open and communicate my feelings and convictions. Encourage me to express my faith.

Learning to Leap

Yea, by thee I can crush a troop, and by my God I can leap over a wall
(II Samuel 22:30).

The red and gray squirrels that occupy our grove scamper through the trees with reckless abandonment. They have athletic feats that would make the finest trapeze artist green with envy. The long bushy tail not only helps for balance when running along branches or telephone wires, but also serves as a drag to slow its descent when falling. The tail has also been used as a parasol in hot weather.

The squirrel is one of the more intelligent rodents. It efficiently stores seeds and nuts in the holes it digs or in the fork of tree branches. However, it is not its memory that enables it to find these food caches later on in the season, but rather its sensitive nose. The squirrel misplaces a fifth of its food. Unwittingly, it plants nuts that will eventually germinate and start new trees. Squirrels are not true hibernators, since their high metabolism makes it difficult for them to store enough fat to sleep through the winter. That is why we see them on cold winter days out searching for their food caches.

I have always enjoyed watching these experts in tree travel. They perform some fantastic maneuvers as they bound from branch to branch. It seems as though they usually jump for a higher branch, and with uncanny accuracy and balance, they attain their goal. But if they do miss, there will be another branch they can catch on the way down. With great confidence, they leap even though there is a risk involved.

As we face life, we are challenged by the squirrel to "go for it." Fifty people over the age of ninety-five were asked in a survey what they would do differently if they could start over again. The answer that came in second place was, "I would risk more." Theodore Roosevelt said, "Far better it is to dare mighty things, to win glorious triumphs, even checkered by failure, than to take rank with those poor spirits who neither enjoy much or suffer because they live in a twilight that knows not victory or defeat."

Jesus talks about a man who received five talents, another who received two, and a third man who received only one. The first two men took risks and invested their talents and doubled them. The third man was cautious, and buried his talent for fear of losing it. The first two were praised, but the third was reprimanded (Matthew 25:14-30).

Robert Browning said, "A man's reach should exceed his grasp, or what is a heaven for."

Humans are something like rubber bands; their use increases only by being stretched. Ralph Pulitzer warned against complacency and the lack of a spirit of adventure: "Monotony is the awful penalty of the careful."

A man who took risks for the sake of the Gospel was the Apostle Paul. During his three missionary journeys, Paul covered some 8,000 miles by land and sea. He suffered beatings, imprisonment, stoning, shipwreck, and disease, but he was driven by the lofty goal of sharing Christ with all people. He even dreamed of going to Spain. If he were constantly looking before leaping, he probably would not have accomplished nearly as much.

There is a humorous story of a man who was checking some cattle in a large pasture. All of a sudden, an enormous bull started to exercise his territorial rights. As he began to charge, the man saw a tree a short distance away. It had a horizontal limb stretching from the trunk about ten feet high. The man ran for the tree and jumped for the limb just as the bull was ready to ram him with its sharp horns. But the man missed! However, he caught the branch on the way down! Most people have more potential than they think. But if they are not willing to leap in faith, they will never discover the possibilities that life has in store for them.

Lord, help me to expect great things from you and attempt great things for you. I need to learn to be less cautious and more courageous.

Do It Quickly

What you are going to do, do quickly (John 13:27).

The cougar is the most powerful and beautiful of the cat family in North America. A large male weighs about as much as an average man. It is designed as an efficient killing machine with jaws like bolt cutters. The cougar exists by eating no food other than meat. Therefore, it must depend on stalking and killing in order to survive.

This magnificent cat slinks around mainly in mountainous areas and remains nearly invisible. While in Victoria, British Columbia, we heard about a cougar that had entered the heart of the city in 1992 that was caught by wildlife control officers in the parking garage of the Empress Hotel. The population of Victoria was 300,000, and yet nobody had seen this cat penetrate the core of the city. The ability of the cougar to move unseen is eerie.

The intelligence and strength of the cougar is evidenced in the fact that it successfully kills eighty percent of the animals it stalks. That compares to a lion feasting on only one in ten animals it stalks and lynx three out of ten. The cougar can take down an elk, which is many times its size.

There is one element in its hunting prowess that is quite surprising. The cougar must get very close to its prey in order to catch it in a single lunge or a very short chase. Otherwise, the chances of success are diminished. A deer can run at top speed for five or six minutes without a pause. One minute to a cougar is a marathon. It must rest for twenty minutes to catch its breath after a minute sprint. The lesson we learn from the cougar is simple—some things must be done quickly to be successful.

At the Last Supper when Jesus had dipped the morsel, he gave it to Judas and said, "What you are going to do, do quickly." The meaning is somewhat puzzling. But maybe it is simply, "The die is cast; your decision has been made. Let's get on with the activity which will lead to the cross."

When Zacchaeus was up in the tree watching Jesus come by, Jesus looked up and said, "Zacchaeus, make haste and come down; for I must stay at your house today" (Luke 19:5). And it is recorded that Zacchaeus did "make haste." Jesus was preparing to go to Jerusalem, and there was no time to waste. The opportunity had to be seized quickly. A man's soul was at stake!

When Jesus knocks at the door of the human heart, a person should respond quickly so new life can be born. "Today, when you hear his voice, do not harden your hearts" (Hebrews 4:7).

You might miss the opportunity of a lifetime if you do not open the door.

Waiting too long for action on our part often leads to a deep freeze from which there will be no thaw. Timing is important—even in telling a joke. Procrastination has often robbed us of that moment which is life-changing. We all need to cultivate the habit of responding quickly to opportunities and obligations.

Oftentimes, the hardest thing in life is making the start. We are going to break a habit, but not until tomorrow. We are going to start a project, but not until a more convenient season. We are going to lift life to a higher level, but not now. We are going to spend more time with children and mates, but not until a time when we are less busy. Opportunity often knocks many times, but it has a way of knocking for the last time also.

Whittier was right: "For all the sad words of tongue or pen, the saddest are these: 'It might have been!' " (Maud Muller, Stanza 53).

Lord, when you have set an open door before me, may I have the determination to go through it rather than loiter in the hallway. Give me the love that will seize opportunities of service to you.

Takers, Not Givers

But we exhort you, brethren, to do so more and more, to aspire to live quietly, to mind your own affairs, and to work with your hands, as we charged you; so that you may command the respect of outsiders, and be dependent on nobody (I Thessalonians 3:11-12).

While we were fishing in Canada a worm-like creature swam with undulating movements of contraction and elongation alongside our boat. It was a leech. It is also called a "blood-sucker," since it is dependent on a host for sustenance. The leech has a disk-like sucker at each end. It has a mouth centered in the front sucker and may also have small teeth. Leeches are popular bait for fishermen.

Most leeches are parasitic. The dictionary describes a parasite as "an organism that grows, feeds, and lives on or in another organism to whose survival it contributes nothing." There are many plants and mosses that are parasitic in nature. One of the most common is the dodder, which is also known by such names as the "love vine" or "strangle-weed." The dodder has no leaves of its own for the manufacturing of its own food. Its thin stems reach out in long tendrils swayed by every breeze until they come in contact with some other plant. They wrap themselves around the host plant and penetrate the bark of their victim with little suckers in order to secure sap. After it begins to suck sap from its succulent victim, the dodder has no need for its own root, so it withers away, along with the plant's lower portions. The dodder at this stage is totally parasitic. There are several species of the dodder vine in America. Some are selective of the plants on which they grow, while others take almost any plant that comes within its reach. The dictionary also has a second meaning to the word parasite: "One who habitually takes advantage of generosity without making any useful return." In ancient Greece, a parasite was one who flattered and amused his host in return for free meals.

Society can easily slip into the mode of a fellowship of parasites. People can develop the repulsive trait of only looking for what they can get without any thought of what they can give. "What is coming to me?" is the battle cry. Billy Graham once said, "We make a living by what we get, but we make a life by what we give." An old Jewish proverb recognizes how a grasping spirit sucks life out of daily relationships. "The leech has two daughters: 'Give, give,' they cry" (Proverbs 30:15a). The volume of "gimme gimme" seems to be increasing in our day.

Evil habits are also parasitic in that they rob people of their decency and self-respect and give nothing in return. Dissipated human beings are left in the wake of drugs, gambling, prostitution, alcoholism, racketeering, and other parasitic perversions.

The pattern that leads to a parasitic lifestyle may be very subtle. For example, garbage dumps and groceries stacked on the shelf of an open cabin in the woods all lead to the development of an uncommon predilection for human foods among bears. Campgrounds put up signs saying, "Don't feed the bears." What happens when we violate that standard is that the bear, rather than foraging for its natural foods, finds it easier to beg or look for human food. A dependency develops, and the bear has evolved into a dangerous freeloader. Receiving handouts without working for our daily bread usually ends in disaster. Too many subsidies will starve the dignity that a man finds only in "paying his own way."

Lord, we get weary and are ashamed of our selfish lives. Forgive our self-centeredness and help us to pray, "Lord, make me what you want me to be" rather than constantly uttering, "Give me."

Pig Potential

Now to him who by the power at work within us is able to do far more abundantly than all we ask or think . . . (Ephesians 3:20).

> The nice little pig with a querly tail,
> All soft as satin and a pinky pale
> Is a very different thing by far
> Than the lumps of iniquity big pigs are.
> (Anonymous)

Many years ago I was presented with a baby pig at a "roast" in my honor. Since we lived on a twenty-six acre plot with a small barn, I proceeded to raise the little piglet until it was large enough to butcher. I discovered through observation and reading that there are many false ideas that have sprung up concerning this animal. Most of the notions are degrading. You hear about the person who eats a large meal: "He is pigging out." A messy house is called "a pig pen." Obesity is synonymous with hog-like proportions. By using these common phrases we are being cruel to people and propagating misinformation about the pig.

The pig is one of the neatest of all farm animals. The idea of a filthy pig comes from the influence of man upon this animal by keeping him in tight surroundings and ill-kept pens. Left alone, the pig keeps its bed clean. Since the pig is sparsely clothed with bristles and hairs, which yield no protection from the attack of flies and other insects, it has learned to take mud baths for the purpose of keeping its body free from vermin. These also cool the body.

The pig has a strange nose which is like a fleshy disc with nostrils in its middle. The nose is a sensitive organ that can distinguish grain from chaff, yet is strong enough to root up the ground in search of food.

The pig's sense of smell is very acute. There are cases in which a pig has been trained as a pointer (dog) for hunting birds. French pigs are taught to hunt for truffles which are grown beneath the soil. It is through the sense of smell that the pig detects their presence.

Some years ago I listened to a discussion on the Johnny Carson show about the comparative intelligence between the horse and the pig. Most seemed to give the pig low ratings. Yet many students of animal behavior will say the pig is perhaps the most intelligent of farm animals. It has an excellent memory and can be taught tricks readily, but keeping the pig penned up and stuffing it with food gives it little opportunity to use its brain. Those who hunt wild hogs have learned that the pig is full of strategy and cunning and can become very fierce. Due to misinformation and pre-conceived ideas we have minimized the real potential of the pig. Our minds have become closed to the possibilities of this animal which we thought was only good for ham, bacon, pork chops, and a few good roasts.

Tragically, this also happens too frequently in our observations of the people around us. We don't look for hidden talents and abilities. We judge by external appearance and mannerisms. We don't give people an opportunity to grow. They get penned in! Oliver Wendell Holmes said, "Most people die with their music still in them." This occurs when we put people down rather than building them up.

Nathaniel totally jumped to the wrong conclusion when Philip told him of Jesus of Nazareth. Nathaniel said, "Can anything good come out of Nazareth?" (John 1:46). He underestimated the possibilities of that small town. Let us not be guilty of underestimating the gifts that God has given our families and neighbors.

Lord, I need to confess that I am way too quick in attempting to evaluate the gifts and talents of those around me. I have misjudged and consequently passed over hidden abilities for which I did not look. Help me to be more of an encourager.

Stay Close To The Power

I can do all things in him who strengthens me (Philippians 4:13).

It was a warm and humid summer evening. The haunting hoot of a great horned owl broke the silence of the night. Stars were twinkling against the dark canopy of the heavens. Suddenly a slight breeze started to whisper through the leafy ash trees. Some clouds began to drift in from the west and the stars faded from view. A few raindrops splattered on our cement driveway. Soon the clouds opened up their faucets, and a summer downpour drenched the earth below. The ground rapidly became soft and saturated.

Following the cessation of the rain, movement began in the soil. The earthworm called the night crawler was coming out of his underground home for an evening stroll with his friends. Some of these worms stayed in the safety of the grass, while others were beckoned by the warmth of our cement driveway, which had been thoroughly heated by the daytime sun.

But for several of the night crawlers, danger approached of which they were not yet aware. They loitered too long on the driveway as dawn quickly came, and the sun and morning breeze dried off the cement surface very rapidly. Without adequate surrounding moisture, the skin of the night crawlers stiffened, and their mobility was hindered. On that summer morning, many of them shriveled and died before reaching their boroughs in the moist ground which would sustain them.

This episode from the world of night crawlers brings to mind a story from Greek mythology. Antaeus was a giant who was the son of the goddess Earth (Gaea). It was his custom to challenge in mortal combat any intruder who passed through his territory. Much to his opponent's dismay, they found that no amount of beating Antaeus against the earth could subdue him. He would merely arise stronger and more refreshed each time he was thrown down. Hercules, the Greek mythical hero, found Antaeus a worthy opponent. During the battle Hercules ascertained the secret of Antaeus' strength. Each time he was thrown to the ground, he gained strength from his mother Earth. With this knowledge, Hercules defeated Antaeus by picking him up, suspending him in mid-air, and squeezing the life out of him. Severed from his source of strength, the giant was defeated.

The night crawler and the story from Greek mythology carries a poignant truth for Christians. We cannot remain strong and alive spiritually if we are detached from our source of power. Jesus said, "I am the true vine. . . . Abide in me and I in you. As a branch cannot bear fruit by itself, unless it abides in the vine, neither can you, unless you abide in me" (John 15:1,4).

Martin Luther aptly describes this in his great Reformation hymn:

No strength of ours can match his might!
We would be lost, rejected.
But now a champion comes to fight,
Whom God himself elected.
You ask who this may be?
The Lord of hosts is he!
Christ Jesus, mighty Lord.
God's only Son, adored.
He holds the field victorious.

In the passion history of our Lord, Peter serves as an example of what happens when the connection to Christ is loosened. It began with a proud boast that he would die before denying Christ. Later in the Garden of Gethsemane, he slept when Jesus asked him to pray. After the betrayal by Judas and the arrest, Scripture says that Peter "followed at a distance" (Luke 22:54). Then came the denial!

Without remaining close to Christ, all of us will fail to remain faithful. We need to keep our connection to Jesus in good condition.

Lord, forgive us from wandering away from you on our little selfish excursions in the far country. Help us to daily declare our dependency on you.

Mimicking Birds

Therefore be imitators of God, as beloved children. And walk in love, as Christ loved us and gave himself up for us, a fragrant offering and sacrifice to God (Ephesians 5:1-2).

While wandering through our tree-filled back yard, I heard a beautiful song filling the air. Immediately I tried to locate the bird from which this delightful sound was arising. Much to my surprise, it was a drab-colored cowbird. It was the first time I realized that some birds can mimic the songs of other birds.

From squeals and discordant sounds to delicate piano notes, there are few sounds that some bird species are not capable of imitating. Whatever might be their reason for being a mimic, they probably have fun in simply expanding their vocal repertoires. In a book by the Discovery Channel entitled *Birds,* it was stated that the marsh warbler has been found to imitate some two hundred European and African species. Many of these songs are picked up during its winter stay in Africa. Another expert mimic is the mockingbird. Its Latin name is Mimus polyglottos, which is very appropriate. There are records of a single mockingbird imitating the calls of three dozen other birds. In another study it was discovered that a crested lark in Germany learned the whistled commands that a shepherd used with his dog. When they recorded the lark's impersonations and played them, the dog obeyed the specific commands. Amazing!

While most people perhaps spend little time imitating the voices of others, there is an abundance of mimicking going on in our society. Young people mimic star athletes and rock singers by wearing their shoe and clothing styles. Many times you see them mimicking the movements and actions of their so-called "idols." The advertising world is also aware that adults can be swayed by the dress and behavior of celebrities.

Mimicking or imitating can be positive or negative. Dr. John P. Kildahl was a well-known psychologist who said that adolescents are more than mimics—they are mirrors. You may often see the parents through their children's lives. Faith for future generations is not only taught by a well-constructed program of parish education, but much of it is "caught" as youth associate with parents and other adults.

Someone once said, "Till a boy is fifteen he does what his father says. After that he does what his father does." There are exceptions to this, of course. Abraham told a half-lie about his wife, saying she was his sister to keep them out of danger. Later Isaac, his son, lied in the same kind of situation about his wife (cf. Genesis 12:10-13; 26;6-16). David took another man's wife in the heat of passion, so it is not surprising to read that his son Ammon violated his sister, and that another son Absolom shacked up with his father's concubines. It is said of many of the kings of Israel and Judah that they walked in the ways of their fathers, whether for good or evil.

Therefore, it behooves all of us to live our lives uprightly and in the light of the Lord. There is a child or an adult who might be mimicking us. Perhaps the most persuasive and eloquent sermons you will ever preach are the daily examples of Christian concern and compassion that are seen by your family and friends.

Paul says, "Be imitators of me, as I am of Christ" (I Corinthians 11:1). And again, "And you became imitators of us and of the Lord, for you received the word in much affliction, with joy inspired by the Holy Spirit; so that you became an example to all the believers in Macedonia and Achaia" (I Thessalonians 1; 6-7).

Dear Lord, may you be the one whom I mimic. May my life, guided by the Holy Spirit, be an inspiration to those who walk with me and by me.

The Amazing Monarch

I will instruct you and teach you the way you should go; I will counsel you with my eye upon you (Psalm 32:8).

When you have an abundance of flowers gracing your gardens you attract beautiful winged visitors. Butterflies of various colors drop by for their afternoon tea, which consists of different flavors of nectar provided by the flower hosts. My favorite visitor is the monarch butterfly. It is decked out in a fine garment of regal orange and outlined in black. Weighing about as much as a paper clip, it flits effortlessly from one bloom to the next.

When the fall season arrives, where does this phantom of the sky disappear? One autumn while living in St. Paul, I received a phone call from a friend who knew I loved nature stories. He told me that he was looking out his window and saw a large mass of butterflies, like a small cloud, floating toward the southwest. "Jim," he said, "they are monarchs heading for Mexico!"

Until some years back, the migration of the monarch was a mystery. But D. Fred Urquhart, zoologist at the University of Toronto, and other colleagues solved the puzzle. These monarchs from the upper midwest were found in the millions wintering in a twenty-acre grove of pine in the Sierra Mountains of Mexico. The temperature there is perfect for the partial hibernation of the monarch, ranging from 42 to 60 degrees Fahrenheit—too warm to freeze and too cold to do much flying. Thus the monarch is in an environment in which it will survive and be able to later perpetuate the species.

When March rolls around, the monarchs mate and head for Texas where the milkweed is ripening. The female lays its eggs—the caterpillar emerges three to twelve days following; it feeds on the milkweed—the chrysalis is formed; and in two weeks the adult butterfly emerges. From egg to adult the process takes about five weeks.

Then it is travel time again. The parent monarchs die along the route to the north. The children arrive in the upper midwest in late May or early June. Of course, right at the time there is a ripening of the milkweed! This generation mates and only lives out a brief life-span of approximately six weeks. Their offspring are born in late August or early September.

Now happen a couple of miracles that only the good Lord could perform. The Mexican monarch's great-grandchildren, who are born in Minnesota in late summer, have a chemical or hormonal change, which gives them a life expectancy of over seven months, in comparison to the six weeks of the previous generations. This enables them to make the 2000-mile flight to the wintering site in Mexico and live there until spring. Imagine that distance being completed by such a small insect with frail wings, buffeted by winds and drenched by rains!

But just as amazing is how they navigate without being blown off course and ending up in the ocean. These monarchs that head south are three generations removed from those who made the trip the previous year. How can they possibly find a small twenty-acre plot nestled in the mountains? They have no maps and no instructional booklet to follow. There is an awesome void in our knowledge of this mystery. I guess only the Creator understands. So far the secret has not been revealed to us, but is locked within the tiny brain of this gorgeous little creature.

What about me, created in the image of God—will I too be guided? Certainly! He is waiting for us to ask directions. William Cullen Bryant wrote these words in a poem, "To a Waterfowl":

He, who, from zone to zone,
Guides through the boundless sky thy certain flight,
In the long way that I must tread alone
Will lead my steps aright
This, too, is a mystery!

Guide me, ever Great Redeemer, through this world in which I live. I am weak, but you are mighty. Hold me with your powerful hand.

Losing Discretion

Then once more you shall distinguish between the righteous and the wicked, between one who serves God and one who does not serve him (Malachi 3:18).

It was a peaceful winter day when I looked out our living room picture window and saw about nine crows perched on the bare limbs of a large ash tree. They seemed a bit nervous since the tree was very close to the house. Their "cawing" sounds indicated that messages were being exchanged. I wondered what they were communicating. One thing was certain: the Lord did not bless them with the ability to harmonize or be melodious.

These jet-black birds are about twenty inches in length. They enjoy congregating and develop a strong group loyalty. The crow has keen eyesight and has an ability to detect anything unnatural in its surroundings. It has learned to cautiously keep its distance from suspicious objects. If shot at, it will quickly learn to stay out of the range of guns. A crow will eat almost anything, from grain and fruits to insects and decaying meat. You will often see these "garbage collectors" along roadsides cleaning up roadkill of rabbits, squirrels, and deer. However, you will seldom see a dead crow, for when a car approaches, it rapidly takes flight with time to spare. The alertness and watchfulness of this bird preserve its existence.

One of my sons, Nathan, has taken a real interest in crows because the bird displays a fairly high intelligence. Like the parrot, the crow can mimic certain words and also learns to respond to simple commands. Over the years, Nathan has raised several crows from the fledgling state to adulthood. He becomes the surrogate mother. But in the process of domesticating the bird, the crow loses its ability to discern between that which is safe or that which is dangerous. The natural instinct of vigilance seems to disappear. A car hit one of the crows he raised as the bird flew out to the road with no fear. After all, he had not been instructed by his peers that big moving objects were detrimental to his health. In another incident, my son had trained a crow to fly down and perch on the back of his German shepherd. The crow evidently thought that all dogs would like him as a friend. He tried that on a neighbor's dog, and his life came to a quick end.

Solomon gave this request to the Lord: "Give thy servant therefore an understanding mind to govern thy people, that I may discern between good and evil, for who is able to govern this great people?" (I Kings 3:9).

There is a word in our language that has fallen into disrepute. The word is "discrimination." Today, it is usually perceived as associated with racism, bias, and prejudice. However, the Oxford English Dictionary traces the understanding of this word back to 1648; for the following 33 years "discrimination" was a virtue, not a vice. Its real meaning was "the ability to tell differences." One of the problems of our modern day is that many issues and behaviors are ambiguous. Society is afraid to make judgments. Right and wrong are not black and white, but a dull gray. In fear of making unfair distinctions, we pretend there are no distinctions to be made.

The writer of Hebrews explains that while a child needs milk, a mature person needs solid food. He says, "But solid food is for the mature, for those who have their faculties trained by practice to distinguish good from evil" (Hebrews 5:14). George Sanchez said, "More and more the line of distinction is being rubbed out between the people of the Kingdom of God and the people who know nothing of his kingdom." Values are blurred between the two. We have lost the ability to discern good from evil. That ability comes from the living Word of God.

Sooner or later, all the crows my son had tamed met their end since they could not differentiate between friends and enemies. When taken from their native wild environment, they were doomed. This also happens when people lose their connection with God and the environment of his Kingdom.

Lord, sometimes I feel like I am living in a twilight zone. There is a moral fog where black and white have become like a dull gray. Sharpen my conscience, **enlighten my mind.**

The Attraction of Light

And I, when I am lifted up from the earth, will draw all men unto myself (John 12:32).

It was a warm October evening, and we were expecting company. Our outdoor porch light was on as a welcome signal. Before our guests arrived, I looked out and saw a swarm of moths fluttering around the light. I knew that trouble lurked closely by. As the guests arrived, the door was opened, and like a squadron of tiny planes, the moths flew into our family room, where a large chandelier hung from the ceiling with glass globes glowing. As the little winged creatures circled about the room, one by one, they flew into one of the open-topped glass globes only to be overcome by the heat. The main job of the next day was to take each globe down and clean out the dead moths.

There are about 75 families of moths. Unlike butterflies, they have feathery antennae without knobs and are mainly nocturnal in habit. Great damage can be done by the larvae (caterpillar stage) of many moths, such as the clothes moth or the gypsy moth. The cocoon of the domesticated silkworm, the source of commercial silk, was one of the main sources of wealth in many ancient Chinese cities.

I wonder what it is about light that attracts moths. Whether it is the inviting appearance of the light or the warmth it radiates, I do not know. Maybe both! But I do know that in the darkness of human history, humankind longs for and is enticed to search for the light. Isaiah says, "The people who walked in darkness have seen a great light ..." (Isaiah 9:2). Light brings hope. The dawn awakens the spirit. If you live in the country and are driving home on a dark and stormy winter night, the first glimpse of the farm light is a welcoming sight. It signifies warmth and safety. It is clever advertising when a national motel chain uses the slogan, "We'll leave the light on!"

It is not by accident that the Scripture says, "This is the message we have heard from him and proclaim to you, that God is light and in him is no darkness at all" (I John 1:15). And Jesus says, "I am the light of the world" (John 8:12).

We, too, search for the light like the moth. And in that light we find life and not death! In it is revealed God's wonderful redeeming love. "Do you not know that God's kindness is meant to lead you to repentance?" (Romans 2:4). Therefore the most powerful teaching and preaching is to center our attention on Jesus, for he is the Light that attracts. Our question must always be: Is the light on? Walter Wangerin wrote his column in "The Lutheran" (September, 1999 issue) on the theme "Jesus, our true center." Part of the column read like this:

> In my traveling I've heard sermons of energy and talent in which Jesus was not the central message: We were. Our niceness was. Our natural human capacity, if only we learned how to access the divine within us. Or else the necessity of justice was the central message. Or the American need of morality was. Or family values was. But not Jesus. Jesus, in fact, was shanghaied to support what the preachers chose as their great truths. I don't blame those issues, nor am I troubled by commitment to them. In themselves they are not bad. But neither do they save. Let them arise from Christ, as Christ is the source of our life and, all our goodness.

Paul put it plainly: "For what we preach is not ourselves, but Jesus Christ as Lord, with ourselves as your servants for Christ's sake. For it is the God who said, 'Let light shine out of darkness,' who has shone in our hearts to give the light of the glory of God in the face of Christ" (II Corinthians 4:6).

Keep the light on . . . and the people will be drawn to it.

Thank you, Lord, that you never turn off the light. Even when we are traveling through a dark tunnel of life, there is the light at the end which gives us strength to continue on. May we let your light shine in us so we may help others on the way.

He Knows Where I Am

If I take the wings of the morning and dwell in the uttermost parts of the sea, even there thy hand shall lead me, and thy right hand shall hold me. (Psalm 139:9-10)

Karsten Isachsen, a pastor in Norway, wrote about a trip he made to the isle of Rost off the northern coast of Norway (Lutheran Standard, January 4, 1985). On the cliffs corralling the coastline, thousands of birds find their nesting spots. Down below, the ocean floor is covered with sharp rocks and reefs, which provide home for teeming fish. Thus, the birds have an ideal dining place below their roosts.

At mid-day the sky is filled with whirling wings, as if a cloud formation has taken shape. The sound emitted is like an endless, feather-clad chorus competing for listeners.

Isachsen visited some researchers who had been coming to the isle for ten years studying the habits of these flying singers of the north. The day he arrived at the research station, they told him that they had fetched a bird's egg from a nest two days before it was ready to hatch. They also marked the mother bird. The egg was then brought to the station, where it was hatched in an incubator.

Several days later they took the week-old chick back to the nesting cliff and placed it in a different area, far from the original nest. Then the researchers hid and waited to see if anything would happen. After a short time, an adult bird broke from the swarm of birds in the sky, dove down to pluck the chick from the foreign nest, and brought it back to where it belonged.

Miraculous, to be sure. But the researchers told Pastor Isachsen that sound-measuring devices have shown that a chick, even before it is hatched, emits its own unique sound, different from that of any other bird. Therefore, among the thousands of birds, the mother bird was able to recognize the sound she had heard earlier from within the egg, sounds made by her unborn chick.

Jeremiah wrote: "The word of the Lord came to me, saying, 'Before I formed you in the womb I knew you, before you were born I set you apart'" (Jeremiah 1:4-5). Jesus spoke of the heavenly Father knowing all about us, by using the imagery of the birds, "Are not two sparrows sold for a penny? And not one of them will fall to the ground without your Father's will. But even the hairs of your head are numbered" (Matthew 19:29-30).

What a blessing to know that you and I are not forgotten and lost in the myriad of people who make their pilgrimage across the earth! To be recognized by the Redeemer is a great reward in itself. The psalmist took great comfort in the realization that God kept watch over his own.

"O Lord, thou hast searched me and known me! Thou knowest when I sit down and when I rise up; thou discernest my thoughts from afar. Thou searchest out my path and my lying down, and art acquainted with all my ways. Even before a word is on my tongue, lo, O Lord, thou knowest it all together . . . Such knowledge is too wonderful for me; it is high, I cannot attain it" (Psalm 139:1-6).

Charles Gabriel wrote a gospel song which affirms this truth:

Why should I feel discouraged,
Why should the shadows come,
Why should my heart be lonely
And long for heaven and home,
When Jesus is my portion?
My constant Friend is He:
His eye is on the sparrow and I know
He watches me.

Abide among us always, Lord, with your faithfulness. O Jesus, never leave us and help us in distress.

The Need for Struggle

I urge you, brothers, by our Lord Jesus Christ and by the love of the Spirit, to join me in my struggle by praying to God for me (Romans 15:30).

Perhaps you have found a cocoon on a tree or in some bushes. You pick it off the branch and wonder what is happening inside that silken capsule. There was a young boy who once found the cocoon of the Cecropia moth. He saw that there was a small opening on one end of the cocoon. It appeared as though the moth was attempting to break out of its casket, but was having great difficulty in doing so. Thus the boy decided to help the process of birth by widening the opening, making it easier for the moth to emerge.

He took his penknife and, ever so carefully, commenced to cut a good-sized slit in the cocoon in order to provide a quick exit for this creature from its imprisonment. Sure enough, the moth emerged into its strange new world. But there was a problem—a big one! Its shriveled wings were wrapped close to its body. The moth appeared frail and feeble. What the boy did not realize was that the struggle to break out of the cocoon was an essential means of developing the muscle system of the moth's body. The pressure of those muscles working together was necessary to push blood into the wings and fill them out to their full dimension. In an effort to relieve the struggle to be born, the boy had unwittingly become an enemy of the moth. He had deprived the moth of the strength that comes only through the struggle of birth. The moth was dead by day's end.

Struggle seems to be God's and nature's way of growth and development. There is an old adage: "The north wind made the Vikings." Fighting the onslaught of the rough seas made the ancient Norwegians into a hearty bunch. Struggle seems to put color in the blood, confidence in the soul, light in the eyes, and steel in the backbone.

There was a pithy, yet somewhat brutal, saying that came out of the westward movement of the pioneers of our country: "The cowards never started, and the weak ones died on the way." Struggle was accepted as necessary in accomplishing the goal of a fresh start in a new, sometimes unforgiving, land.

Arnold Toynbee, the great English historian, said, "It is difficulties and obstacles that lead to the flowering of a civilization." Perhaps that is true of individuals also. Taking the easy, well-worn path may not lead us to the fulfillment of our true potential. Rivers are crooked because they follow the path of least resistance. Lives may often get crooked in the same way. George Gray Barnard, a noted sculptor, said, "For only through constant struggle do we grow or attain victory. The struggle in life is the important thing."

For decades in this past century, men dreamed of running a mile in fewer than four minutes. Roger Bannister, a runner and also a physician in England, was clocked many times at close to four minutes flat, but the barrier was not broken. He approached the goal as a scientist with studied effort. He discovered that the body had to be put through a rigorous weight-lifting program to develop strength to endure the pain if the four-minute mile were to be achieved. He subjected himself to that stress and was the first human to run the mile in less than four minutes. Presently, many runners are under the four-minute mark.

James writes, "Dear brothers, is your life full of difficulties and temptations? Then be happy, for when the way is rough, your patience has a chance to grow, and don't try to squirm out of your problems. For when patience is finally in full bloom, then you will be ready for anything, strong in character, full and complete" (James 1:2-4 TLB).

Lord, forgive me for always looking for an easier life. Help me to accept difficult challenges that will enable me to grow to spiritual maturity.

Thorns and Thistles

Cursed is the ground because of you; in toil you shall eat of it all the days of your life; thorns and thistles it shall bring forth (Genesis 3:17-18).

In the field around our pond we have a healthy growth of thistles. In the summertime they sprout attractive purple flowers. They seem quite innocent. But when autumn arrives and you walk through a patch of thistles, you will be annoyed by the number of prickly burs that stick to your pants. As you attempt to pull them off, the sharp, needle-like projections prick your fingers. If your long-haired dog strolls through the thistle weeds, you will have great difficulty removing the burrs, since they become matted in the hair very quickly. No one appreciates thistles or cockleburs or other obnoxious weeds, which seem to enjoy attaching to us when we saunter through their area.

Thorns belong in the same category of things we don't like. If you have ever cut down Russian olive bushes or locust tree branches you will know what I mean. Their sharp thorns will pierce your skin, and you will be the recipient of bloody scratches. Even the beautiful rose will let you know the sharp pain of a good jab if you pick up the stem in the wrong way.

How are we to look upon thorns and thistles? Are they all bad? Yes and no. Certainly they are like pests, and they mess up a field of grain or a garden. Yet the gorgeous little yellow finch enjoys the thistle seeds in my summer bird feeder. These tiny seeds are the finch's favorite food. And a patch of brier bushes make a wonderful place for the cottontail rabbit to takes cover from its predators.

We must learn to live with thorns and thistles for they are here to stay. Accidents, sickness, job loss, bad weather, and other unpleasant happenings are similar to thorns and thistles. How we handle them is the crux of the matter. Harry Emerson Fosdick once made the acute observation that Jesus never said he had explained the world; he said he had overcome it. The Apostle Paul had a troublesome problem, which is not fully disclosed. He said, "And to keep me from being too elated by the abundance of revelations, a thorn was given to me, a messenger of Satan to harass me, to keep me from being too elated. Three times I besought the Lord about this, that it should leave me; but he said to me, 'My grace is sufficient for you, for my power is made perfect in weakness'" (II Corinthians 12:7-9). Paul attempted to understand the "why" of this thorn, which he was experiencing. He called it a "messenger of Satan" and decided it must be for the purpose of keeping him humble.

When he asked God for release from this thorn in the flesh, he received only a simple answer: that he should live with it, and God's grace would enable him to do just that. God never told him why the thorn pierced his body.

In our Protestant tradition, the mystery of God and his doings are often a cause for analysis and explanation. We get uncomfortable with mystery and attempt to expunge it by finding answers at the bar of reason. Our Orthodox friends can bask in the mystery and transcendence of God without always searching for an explanation. One does not have to know all the answers to live effective lives. Thorns and thistles may indeed provide a lesson for us to learn.

God hath not promised   *But God hath promised*
Skies always blue.   *Strength for the day,*
Flower strewn pathways   *Rest for the labor,*
All our lives through;   *Light for the way,*
God hath not promised   *Grace for all trials,*
Sun without rain.   *Help from above,*
Joy without sorrow.   *Unfailing sympathy*
Peace without pain.   *Undying love.*

Annie Johnson Flynt

Lord, you don't always give me what I want, but I know you will supply me with what I need. Help me to be satisfied with that.

Rabbits Run

Flee the evil desires of youth and pursue righteousness, faith, love and peace, along with those who call on the Lord out of a pure heart (II Timothy 2:22 NIV).

The stories of Peter Rabbit and Br'er Fox have intrigued children for many years. The fox was always trying to catch the mischievous rabbit. The farmer was also in pursuit of the rabbit, since the pesky little thief was continually invading his vegetable garden.

Rabbits are frequent squatters on the twenty-six acres where we live. These rabbits are called cottontails and are a nuisance as they cause much destruction to vegetable and flower gardens. In the winter they eat the bark off many young trees and bushes. The cottontail is prolific in reproduction. The young are born blind and helpless in a shallow hole the mother has dug and lined with her own fur.

The hind legs of the rabbit are larger than the front ones. This enables it to jump start and be off running at a good speed. When a person or a predator approaches, the rabbit sits very still, hoping not to be seen. But when closer than twenty-six to thirty feet, the rabbit bounds away for cover. Since they are preyed upon by hunters as well as owls, eagles, foxes, and coyotes, few cottontails in the wild will live to see their second birthday.

A larger rabbit in our area is the hare, commonly called the jackrabbit. They live in the open prairie where there is no place to hide. Their only escape is their speed. They are built for running with oversized back legs. The jackrabbit has been clocked at forty miles per hour and can make sharp course changes that make it difficult for the predator to catch it. Consequently, they usually survive longer than the cottontails. The young hares are born in the open grasslands with their eyes open. They can be up and running within a few hours after birth.

Since rabbits have no defense equipment, their only hope of survival is their ability to run. There are times when Christians are called upon to stand firm and fight the forces of evil, but there are also times when running may be the wisest action. It is not always a sign of cowardice to run.

Sodom and Gomorrah were wicked cities. Lot and his family were visited by two angels and told about the coming destruction of the towns and were commanded: "Flee for your life; do not look back or stop anywhere in the valley" (Genesis 19:17). Lot's wife looked back and became a pillar of salt. Fleeing was the only way of escape.

Potiphar's wife repeatedly tried to seduce the young handsome Joseph. One day she grabbed his garment as he fled the premises. The scorned woman framed Joseph, but he was later vindicated. Fleeing was his best option (Genesis 30).

Jesus, the Good Shepherd, says his sheep will not follow false gods. "A stranger they will not follow, but they will flee from him, for they do not know the voice of strangers" (John 10:5).

Young people are frequently invited to parties. When they arrive they may discover that alcohol and drugs are being used. What is the best advice for a Christian? Stay there and attempt to be a good witness? No, the best policy is to leave immediately. To run! That, too, is a witness. Paul says, "Flee from sexual immorality". . . (I Corinthians 6:18 NIV). Temptation is not to be played with, for it can consume you. Dag Hammarskjold said, "You cannot play with the animal in you without becoming wholly animal, play with falsehood without forfeiting your right to truth, play with cruelty without losing your sensitivity of mind. He who wants to keep his garden tidy doesn't reserve a plot for weeds."

Lord, I'm slow to learn that you cannot play with fire without getting burned. Give me wisdom to flee that which destroys my relationship with you and others who are dear to me.

Touch Me

And he took a child, and put him in the midst of them; and taking him in his arms. . . (Mark 9:36).

There is a universal longing among all young mammals to rub against the bodies of their mothers and siblings. Female animals often lick their young. We have often thought it was in order to keep them clean. However, it performs a much more profound purpose. It stimulates the body, which is essential for their organic and behavioral development.

Our golden Labrador spends most of her time leisurely roaming around in her fenced pen. When I approach the gate to release her for some exercise time, she gets very excited and begins to jump around like a hopping frog. As soon as the gate is half open she bolts out into the field. She runs about thirty to forty feet, spins around, and runs back to me for a quick stroke or two on her head. Off she goes again, only to retreat once more for a quick petting session. Even though she wants time to run free with the wind, the insatiable desire to be stroked takes precedence.

Our fluffy, snow-white cat spends a lot of time sitting on the ledge outside our kitchen window. She rubs against the window when we are close as though our touch could travel through the glass pane. Often when we are outside, she will run a few steps ahead of us and then roll over on the sidewalk. In silent language she is requesting a scratch. When that is administered, she will purr as if in ecstasy.

These two pets are not ashamed or inhibited about asking for the touch that communicates love and acceptance. It is also a powerful stimulant to the body and mind of the animal.

Adult humans are usually more inhibited in demonstrating a need to be touched. They will go for long lengths of time experiencing a starvation diet instead of the food of touch for their skin hunger. Infants usually receive a good dosage of the medicine of touching. The child is cradled in the parents' arms, caressed and cooed to very frequently. This fondling is affirming, growth-enhancing, and healing. But as the years go by there is often a diminishing of the reinforcing power of touch. Both youth and adults are the poorer because of it.

In our culture, touching has become off-limits, due in part to sexual harassment charges and the mixed messages of intimacy. The social pressure in America has eliminated much normal touching. Italians and the French may touch each other a hundred times in an hour of conversation. Americans make contact fewer than three times.

I was raised in a home where there was an ample supply of love being shown in many ways. However, when we three boys grew up, the expression of love was largely channeled into verbal communication and hand shaking. Hugging was more rare. It was not until my father had died and my mother was later suffering from a paralyzing stroke that the barrier of reserved expression broke down. I began hugging my mother and giving her kisses. I wish I had started doing that long before. The love was always there, but the physical expression punctuated it in a way where words fell short. In the process I discovered that I needed to receive it as well as give it. William James wrote, "Never suffer yourself to have an emotion without giving active expression to it."

Often in Scripture we see Jesus touching those whom he healed. He took the little children in his arms and blessed them. When Paul said farewell at the seaport of Miletus to elders of the church in Ephesus, it says, "He knelt down with all of them and prayed. They all wept as they embraced him and kissed him" (Acts 20:36-37).

Thank you, Lord, that when you were on earth you reached out and touch lonely and suffering people, showing them that you cared. Teach me to give concrete expression to my caring.

The Need For Armor

Let us then cast off the works of darkness and put on the armor of light (Romans 13:12).

As small boys we sometimes pretended to engage in battle like the knights of old. The best shield we could find was the cover of an old garbage can. The sword was never made of steel, but a three to four foot tree branch or stick of wood worked just fine. We would swing heartily at one another, but were always intent on striking the shield of the opponent. It was usually a harmless contest, unless one missed the garbage can cover and hit the competition with a direct blow. If that happened, the game was quickly over.

Shields in earlier days were used to fend off the enemy by diverting the strikes of swords or spears. They also protected against the onslaught of arrows. Presently, riot police face unruly crowds by using shields to ward off rocks and other thrown objects. A shield is the main piece of armor to protect a person from a frontal attack.

The turtle is a creature that has employed a shield of armor over the eons of time. It is a good thing that turtles have the protective armor of a hard shell since these reptiles are incapable of outrunning even the slowest of predators. In most species the shell is strong enough to guard it from the jaws of its enemies, which are many times its size. When threatened, the turtle draws in its head, legs, and tail and the predator is faced with a tough nut to crack. The turtle might be flipped over, and then it simply waits until the predator gives up and leaves. The turtle will then right itself and slowly continue on its way. This shield has served it well, so it has never had to change its strategy or design.

We, too, have adversaries and need some protective armor. Paul says, "We are not contending against flesh and blood, but against the principalities, against the powers, against the world rulers of this present darkness, against the spiritual hosts of wickedness in the heavenly places" (Ephesians 6:11-12). But God has not left us defenseless against the opposition. He has supplied us with armor sufficient for the battle.

Paul states it in this way, "Therefore take the whole armor of God, that you may be able to withstand in the evil day, and having done all, to stand. Stand therefore, having girded your loins with truth, and having put on the breastplate of righteousness, and having shod your feet with the equipment of the gospel of peace; besides all these, taking the shield of faith, with which you can quench all the flaming darts of the evil one. And take the helmet of salvation and the sword of the Spirit, which is the word of God" (Ephesians 6:13-17).

As the turtle is completely covered by his armor, so God makes available to us all the equipment needed to stand against the forces of evil, which Martin Luther says, "are seeking to devour us."

Perhaps the greatest destructive force of sin is unbelief. The only cure is faith. We are justified by faith, and that is a gift from God. We can't produce it, for it comes through the work of the Holy Spirit. Paul says it is faith that is the shield that diverts the arrows of Satan.

This shield of faith does not guarantee that we will never fail, but that we will be protected from pessimism that paralyzes the soul. The shield does not ward off all injury of body or mind, but will spare us from giving birth to a spirit of revenge or resentment. In the face of pain, we will not wallow in self-pity and complaint. When the winds of adversity blow, we will not cringe in cynicism. In the face of confrontation, we will be guarded from cowardice. When success comes, the shield of faith snuffs out deadly vanity and self-conceit. And when the darkness of death approaches, the shield will cast off the darts of doubt with the hope of the resurrection.

The turtle lives a full life as long as its armor is intact. The people of God will have a full life here and in eternity when they wear the armor God has supplied in Jesus Christ.

Forgive me, Lord, when I act as though there is no battle going on in the world or in my own soul. Help me to recognize the enemy who seeks to destroy my faith. May I take up the whole armor of God that I might stand firm.

Powerful Waters

But let justice roll down like waters, and righteousness like an ever-flowing stream (Amos 5:24).

Rivers have great power. Have you ever stood on the edge of the Grand Canyon and looked down into those abysmal depths? It is a sight of strange and wondrous shapes that seem to continually change color. How was it all formed? They say that the muddy Colorado River seen at the bottom of the great canyon, flowing through the centuries and millennia of time, cut that mighty phenomenon out of the earth's surface.

Have you ever watched a river overflow its banks and invade the surrounding landscape? When fed by the quick melting of winter's heavy snowfall or by a flash flood, there is a devastating force that carries cars, homes, and everything else with it.

Take a trip to Niagara Falls and listen, see, and feel the cascading water fall from great heights to the river below. The spray springs high into the air and makes rainbows in the sun's rays. The roar of the waters is like that of a huge locomotive barreling down the railroad tracks. You feel the majestic power of nature as you stand viewing this spectacular waterfall. You are wrapped in awe.

Amos, the prophet, had seen water rushing down the hillside, tumbling, churning, and moving constantly. It could not stand still. It drove forward as if its life depended on getting somewhere fast. Its movement was somehow like Paul Tillich's description of time in The Shaking of the Foundation: "Time does not return, nor repeat itself; it runs forward; it is always unique; it ever creates the new. There is within it a drive toward an end, unknown, never to be reached in time itself, always intended and ever fleeing." As Amos sat and watched those powerful, moving streams, his mind wrestled with the society in which

he lived. Society had become stagnant with corruption and needed to be cleansed. It had become an abomination to God, and Amos was sure God was not going to stand idly by. Judgment was impending. So Amos cried out in the imagery of nature: "But let justice roll down like waters, and righteousness like an ever-flowing stream."

Amos was a layman who lived on the Tekoan plateau southeast of Jerusalem. He made his living herding sheep and gathering figs. His business took him to the northern markets, where he sold his wool and fruit. There he was astonished at the dissolute life that he witnessed.

He saw that people were confusing religious ritual with righteousness. They were substituting ceremony for conduct. Businessmen were taking advantage of the poor. Scales were being tinkered with. Women wanted their husbands to earn more to pay for bills from the beauty parlor. Life was sensual and selfish, and Amos wanted the waters of justice and righteousness to clean up the mess that humanity had made. Society needed a powerful wash job.

Martin Luther King, Jr. said, "A religion that professes a concern for the souls of men and is not equally concerned about the slums that damn them, the economic conditions that strangle them, and the social conditions that cripple them, is a spiritually moribund religion." The demons once cried to Jesus, "What have you to do with us, Jesus of Nazareth?" The answer is, "Plenty." The worlds of politics, science, and the humanities also frequently phrase the same question: "What have you to do with us?" Jesus has to do with all of life, for the righteousness and justice of God must flow right down Main Street and even into the alleys where trash is stored.

The farmer who is out plowing and the nurse checking your pulse are both under God's surveillance. The architect designing a building and the athlete batting a ball are both responsible to God's calling. Everyone is under his scrutiny, as he demands right and just behavior. "If you know that he (Jesus) is righteous, you may be sure that everyone who does right is born of him" (I John 2:29).

Lord, I must admit that my faith has too often been mainly exercised in the confines of the church. May your Spirit drive me out into the streets of life where human deeds of justice need to be demonstrated.

Room to Expand

And Jesus increased in wisdom and stature, and in favor with God and man (Luke 2:52).

A tall stately elm stood like a sentinel on duty. Straight and erect in stature, it commanded the attention of all those who came by. The trunk was three feet in diameter and held a crown of green foliage that was shaped like a giant puffball. Ten feet from the base of the domineering elm was a struggling oak tree fighting for its life. It was bent over, growing almost horizontally, as it attempted to reach out and grab a beam of sunlight. The power of heliotropism was very evident in this little tree. This is the innate need of a tree or plant to search for the light of the sun so the process of photosynthesis may take place. Sunlight is its source of energy, which enables the tree or plant to take carbon dioxide, water and inorganic salts to combine in order to bring about growth.

Being denied good exposure to sunlight, the oak tree was stunted. The large elm tree had laid claim to the territory and held the younger tree in submission. The oak could never reach its full potential while living in the presence of the giant elm.

Life presents many situations in which people are held back from maximizing their abilities. Oliver Wendell Holmes stated, "Many people die with their music still in them." This happens when a person is not given opportunity to explore and is put down rather than given encouragement to expand his or her horizons. Constant criticism causes people to crawl into themselves and drains dignity from them. Compliments will draw out the best in people. American pioneer psychologist William James said, "The deepest principle in human nature is the craving to be appreciated." It is necessary for growth. When the

Lord talked about the exiles from Judah, he said, "I will build them up, and not tear them down" (Jeremiah 24:6).

The apostle Paul was a giant in the expansion of the Christian faith. He was passionate about sharing Christ and was perhaps a bit impatient when others failed to reach the height of his commitment and stature. On his first missionary journey, he took along Barnabus and young John Mark. When the journey became difficult, John Mark turned back and went home. On Paul's second missionary effort, John Mark requested another opportunity to go along. Paul denied it. He did not tolerate failure, so he was not going to give John Mark a second chance to grow and prove himself. Fortunately, Barnabus, whose name means "son of encouragement," was more understanding. He chose to go on a mission trip with John Mark rather than with Paul. He wanted to give John Mark another chance. Young John Mark did grow as he earned "his wings" in the missionary movement. Later, when Paul was in prison, he recognized that the young man had achieved maturity, and Paul asked for a visit from John Mark.

Recently I viewed a program on Charles Lindberg on the Biography Channel. When Lindberg became the first to fly across the Atlantic, he became a national hero. Coming back from Paris, he flew from city to city, promoting aviation. He flew to Mexico City for the State Department and there met a young lady whose father was ambassador to Mexico. Her name was Anne Morrow, and she, like her husband to be, was somewhat shy and retiring. However, while living under the shadow of a giant hero who was recognized wherever he went, he gave her room to grow. She went on to become one of America's most popular writers. She gave a clue to her success in her career: it was simply that her husband believed in her to an extraordinary degree. She said, "The sheer fact of finding myself loved was unbelievable and changed my world, my feelings about life, and myself. I was given confidence, strength, and almost a new character. The man I was to marry believed in me and what I could do, and consequently I found I could do more than I realized."

Perhaps we all need to pray that God will give us the ability to see good things in unexpected places and talents in unexpected people.

Lord, in the company of sinners you dreamed of saints. Help me to see the best in others and tell them so. May I be an encourager and not a discourager.

Two Different Lives

Do not marvel that I said to you, "You must be born anew "(John 3:17).

On quiet summer evenings our pond becomes a concert hall for the croaking calls of countless frogs. In the daytime, the vocalization diminishes. In the late summer our spacious lawn becomes the playground for many frogs, some of whom become victims of our riding lawnmower.

Frogs belong to that classification called amphibians. Frogs lay their eggs in the water, and when they hatch, tadpoles are the result. The tadpole has a streamlined body that is little more than a head and tail. They are built to swim rapidly and have gills that take in oxygen directly from the water.

As the tadpole grows, its body undergoes a metamorphosis in preparation for its second life as a frog. It develops limbs for climbing, hopping, and swimming. The gills are traded for lungs so it can breathe out of the water. Its mouth grows to almost the width of the body. Some frogs in dry areas can sit in a shallow puddle and absorb water through their skin on their underside, which is highly absorbent.

The calls from the frogs on a summer night are made by shunting air back and forth between their lungs and the extensible throat sacs. If you watch a frog croaking, you will be able to detect the bulging of the elastic throat sac as the air pressure builds up. Why are they making noise? The male frogs vocalize for the same reason as an elk bull bugles or a robin sings. They call females to mate and warn other males to keep their distance. Since there are several species of frogs, each has their distinctive call so they can communicate with their own.

As adults, frogs are among the world's best ambush hunters, catching food with a minimum of movement. They can squat on their folded legs for hours, waiting motionless for insects to approach. Their large eyes near the top of their heads easily focus on their prey. When the prey comes by, the strike is a flick of the tongue with almost no other body movement.

The frog gives us a lesson on a new creature for a new life. The tadpole cannot live like a frog until there is a change in its very being and makeup. Nicodemus, a Pharisee and a member of the Sanhedrin, came to see Jesus late one night because he wondered about spiritual matters and who Jesus really was. Jesus brought him abruptly face to face with the central fact that if the new life in the Kingdom of God is ever to be lived, there must be a new creature. The new creature must be fully new and not a mere tinkering with the outward characteristics of life.

Jesus said, "Truly, truly, I say to you, unless one is born anew he cannot see the kingdom of God" (John 3:3). Nicodemus could not fully understand this, so he asked how a grown man could crawl into his mother's womb and be born again. Nicodemus missed the spiritual implication of being born anew. Jesus told him this miracle of new birth is brought about by the work of the Holy Spirit.

Walter Lippman once wrote that experience has proved Christ is absolutely right; that even with the best will in the world, "the unregenerate man can only muddle into the muddle." Another man said, "No clever arrangement of bad eggs will make a good omelet." The Apostle Paul was the supreme example of the complete change in life when Jesus came in to rebuild his life from the inside out. A persecutor of Christians became the greatest missionary of all time. He wrote: "Therefore, if anyone is in Christ Jesus, he is a new creation; the old has passed away, behold, the new has come" (II Corinthians 5:17).

Nicodemus must have experienced this after his encounter with Jesus. After Christ was crucified, Nicodemus and Joseph of Arimathea asked for permission from Pilate to give Jesus a proper burial. By doing this Nicodemus jeopardized his standing with the Sanhedrin and identified himself as one who admired and reverenced Christ. The whole point of the Gospel is that God can do just that for anyone–for you and me. And he does do it.

Lord, sometimes I don't want a total remodeling job done on my life. I only want a few minor repairs. Help me to see that I'll never be satisfied until I allow you to make me a new creation.

Thinking Ahead

On the first day of every week, each of you is to put something aside and store it up, as he may prosper, so that contributions need not be made when I come (I Corinthians 16:2).

It was the fall of the year, and I was perched high up on a tree stand keeping watch for a black bear. Time moved slowly. Leaves occasionally tumbled by on their descent to the forest floor. In the distance, some crows cawed with their monotonous-sounding voices. Below me, there were several chipmunks in their striped suits busily preparing for winter. They scampered to and fro as though driven by some sense of urgency.

This energetic resident of the woods makes its home in an organized network of tunnels and underground chambers. The tunnel is about two inches in diameter and could reach a depth of four to five feet. There are three to six storage compartments, a bedroom area, and a toilet area. The tunnel always has two openings so the chipmunk can escape out the back door when chased by a predator.

In summer and early fall, the chipmunk is caught up in frenzied activity storing seeds and nuts for its winter treat. It fills the warehouse chambers in the tunnel. The chipmunk does not actually hibernate as bears do, but sleeps and then wakes up when hungry. Then it runs to a storage chamber and has a meal. All its needs are met in its tunnel system since it has made early and methodical provision for its winter retirement. If the chipmunk did not think and plan ahead, the long winter would claim the life of the little creature.

A man was standing on the deck of a large ocean liner. The prow of the ship was cutting through the high waves. He asked a sailor, standing nearby, how far the ship would go before it could stop if it were going at full speed.

The sailor replied, "She couldn't even slow down in less than a mile. It would take more than that to stop. You see, with a big ship like this one, you have to think miles ahead."

That is also true as we sail through the sea of life. We need to think and plan ahead. Many tragedies and failures in life happen because of "spot thinking." We consider the immediate with no concern about the future. Indulging in drugs and alcohol may bring immediate gratification, but this kind of behavior runs into a dead-end street. Pre-marital sex may be thrilling, but may subtract from the beauty of a happy marriage. A person who drops the baton of faith does not think ahead to when he runs the last lap uncheered by faith and hope.

One of the great stories of wisely thinking ahead is found in the Old Testament. It is the account of Nehemiah who was cupbearer to King Artaxerxes of Persia. The walls of Jerusalem had been destroyed, and Nehemiah felt led by God to return to his homeland and rebuild the city. He did not go to the king with a request for a leave of absence without first of all developing a plan. He had been praying for months. When Nehemiah presented his case, King Artaxerxes wanted to know how long the journey would take and when Nehemiah would return. Nehemiah did not hesitate as a man who had not thought of a timetable. He confidently said, "I set him a time" (Nehemiah 2:6). Then he asked the king for a letter (like a passport) to give to the governor through whose providences he would pass. He also asked for the rights to secure timber from the keeper of the king's forests. Nehemiah had a practical mind. The plans were so deliberately made that the venture was sure to be a success. A life well lived is something like a chess match—you must be patient and think many moves ahead.

Lord, help me to look ahead and see the consequences of wrong attitudes and actions. Then show me the delights that lie on the road ahead when I follow your commandments.

A Healthy Coat

I will greatly rejoice in the Lord, for my soul shall exult in my God; for he has clothed me with the garment of salvation, he has covered me with the robe of righteousness (Isaiah 61:10).

The coyote is a smaller version of the timber wolf. The range of coyotes has spread from coast to coast in North America. In the northern plains, the coyote develops a beautiful coat of fur, which at one time was prized by trappers. The intelligence of this animal is very high, and its cunning aptitude has enabled the coyote to frequently avoid traps and poison. With a sprint of forty miles per hour, he can chase down hares. The diet of the coyote is varied. Rabbits and rodents are usually the main course, but coyotes will also eat fish, fruits, frogs, and lizards, and when in the proximity of larger cities, will even eat small dogs and cats.

While hunting elk in the Castle Mountains of Montana, we occasionally saw a coyote. The ranchers do not have a fondness for these animals, since they prey upon young lambs. Therefore, if we saw a coyote, we were encouraged to shoot it in order to keep down the population. On this particular hunt, we had come down from the higher mountain area, and while driving on the road leading to the ranch, we observed a lone coyote evidently stalking a mouse out in the field. The coyote was felled by a rifle shot, but we were very disappointed when we saw his pelt. The fur was thin and matted, and there were scabs on his body where he had been scratching.

The problem was mange. It is a contagious skin disease of domestic and wild animals caused by minute parasitic mites. These mites burrow into the skin, hair follicles, and sweat glands. The mange doesn't necessarily cause death, but in the northern climate, with no warm coat of fur, the coyote will succumb to exposure and freeze to death. Sometimes an outbreak of mange among coyotes will thin out the population more than any other means of control.

This incident in Montana caused me to reflect on the need for proper clothing. When I was a child leaving for school in the winter, my mother had many instructions: "Eat all your cereal because you need energy on this cold day. Put on your sweater for the schoolroom might be chilly. Wear your boots because it snowed three inches last night. Put on your mittens and cap, and don't forget the scarf because the wind is blowing hard this morning." I left for school bundled like a mummy, but I was warm and protected from the cold. Such is the love of a parent.

As a loving parent, God also provides the proper clothing for us. He does so in order to protect us from the evil climate that could easily be our undoing. As I obediently wore what my mother encouraged me to put on, so we, as God's children, should obediently wear the apparel He recommends. "Clothe yourselves, all of you, with humility toward one another . . . " (I Peter 5:5).

"Put on then, as God's chosen ones, holy and beloved, compassion, kindness, lowliness, meekness, and patience, forbearing one another and, if one has a complaint against another, forgiving each other; as the Lord has forgiven you, so you also must forgive. And above all put on love, which binds everything together in perfect harmony. And let the peace of Christ rule in your hearts, to which indeed you were called in the one body" (Colossians 3:12-15). And most importantly, he gives us the coat of righteousness, which is our salvation!

Dear Lord, wrap me in the blanket of your love and providence. Help me to wrap others with kindness and forgiveness so they will experience the warmth of your loving grace.

Coping with Change

And we all, with unveiled face, beholding the glory of the Lord, are being changed into his likeness from one degree of glory to another; for this comes from the Lord who is the Spirit (II Corinthians 3:18).

There is a slap of sadness as well as a jab of joy that comes with autumn leaves. They signal that summer is slipping away and winter is ready to rush in. The God of nature splashes the hillsides with splendid color. He takes his paintbrush and makes skillful strokes across his earthly canvas. The blazing sumacs, flaming maples, and blushing red oaks parade down the autumnal trail with their gaudiest apparel of the year. Henry Thoreau ("Autumnal Tints") says that leaves teach us how to die. "How beautifully they go to their graves! . . . Printed of a thousand hues . . . they troop to their last resting place, light and frisky. . . scampering over the earth."

We sigh as the season ends. Nature seems naked except for the evergreen trees that refuse to shed their clothes. But as the season sweeps by, we get a glimpse of the Creator. Nature affords us a view of the hem of God's garment and gives us a hint of life itself. The swish and swirl of colored leaves carry a sermonette of great significance.

The tree stands firm as the leaves fall. Falling leaves are not fatal to the tree. Man's faith, rooted in the promises of God, also stands firm as the leaves of new life replace the faded leaves of old habits and pious platitudes. There must be a shedding of the past to make room for the sprouting of the future buds of new life.

This law of life is very evident in the physical development of the body. Physiologists say that the body grows by death and rebirth of tissue. The body sloughs off its fingernails every few months. Eyebrows change every one hundred and fifty days. With the exception of the enamel on the teeth, the body replaces itself every seven years. In all growth there seems to be the elements of death as well as of life.

To be deciduous like the trees is to discard, not destroy. To shake the leaves from the tree is far different from felling the tree itself. A faith that is deciduous leaves room for growth. Ideas and behaviors which are no longer tenable are dropped. This, in no way, means the destruction of the tree of faith. Paul said, "When I was a child, I spoke like a child, I thought like a child, I reasoned like a child; when I became a man, I gave up childish ways" (I Corinthians 13:11).

Jesus talked about it in the Sermon on the Mount. He said, "Do not think that I have come to abolish the Law or the Prophets; I have not come to abolish them but to fulfill them" (Matthew 5:17). Rules and regulations were sometimes getting in the way of a real and vital relationship to Jesus Christ, the foundation and center of our faith. People wanted the security of the old rather than the risk of the new. Now we must say that all change does not necessarily mean improvement, but without change there will be no improvement. Paul says that in Christ, "the old has gone, the new has come" (II Corinthians 5:17).

In the days of Jesus, the tree of Judaic faith was groaning under the weight of so many layers of leaves that it was necessary to shake some loose in order to prepare for a time of new greening. The church in every generation needs to grasp the principal of deciduousness.

Lord, I am reluctant to change my old patterns and often reject new ideas which may enhance my life. Help me to be more flexible and not so rigid that I might be open to the leading of your spirit.

The Need to Cut

He cuts off every branch in me that bears no fruit . . . (John 15:2).

Ever since I was a small boy I have been fascinated by the red fox, which roamed the countryside where I grew up. The red fox is the world's most widespread carnivore. It is an intelligent animal, which learns about its terrain and knows how to outwit its would-be adversaries by drawing from its reservoir of tricks.

The red fox has a very keen nose coupled with an uncanny ability to hear. If conditions are favorable, it can hear the faint squeak of a mouse as far as one hundred feet away. A major portion of the fox's diet is composed of rabbits, woodchucks, ground squirrels, and mice. The red fox is blessed with good speed and easily reaches twenty-six miles an hour. Its tail is a thing of beauty. The graceful, fluffy tail with its white tip not only enhances the animal, but also aids the fox in maintaining balance when turning corners at high speeds. Also, on cold winter nights the tail becomes a muffler preventing frostbite as the fox draws itself into a ball and wraps its tail around its exposed nose and footpads. Over the years, the red fox has gained a reputation for being sly and crafty and because of those qualities it thrives today.

When fur prices were high, there were hunting and trapping pressures on the red fox. It has a beautiful coat. I still vividly remember a story related to me by a trapper. It was winter, and he was making the rounds of his extensive trap line. Mink and fox were what he desired to catch. This particular morning there was excitement in the air, for he had gotten two beautiful mink and now was heading for traps baited for the crafty red fox. He saw some tracks that headed toward one of the traps. His heart beat with anticipation! But as he arrived at the trap, disappointment spread across his face. The only thing in the closed teeth of the trap was a portion of a fox's front leg.

Evidently the fox, knowing it could not spring open the trap, decided to gnaw off its leg. He would be crippled for life, but at least he would be alive. With his cunning, he could survive with three good legs. The trapper felt a sting of remorse coupled with great admiration at the courage of this little red-coated animal.

Cutting something off is usually painful, but many times necessary. Jesus talks of cutting off branches that do not bear fruit. The writer of Hebrews encourages us to "lay aside every weight and sin which clings so closely . . ." (Hebrews 12:1). Good and evil do not mix well together. They must be separated. If something or someone is destroying your relationship with God or dimming your vision of goodness and righteousness, it must be terminated. The cutting off may be a radical procedure.

In the movie business, when a producer is not satisfied with the way a scene is shaping up, he will call for the cameraman to "cut." The acting stops, corrections are made, and then the cameras will start rolling again. You cannot continue with a bad performance. This decision to "cut" is also essential in the drama of life. A person must be able to say, "NO." Jesus said, "If your right hand causes you to sin, cut it off and throw it away; it is better that you lose one of your members than your whole body go into hell" (Matthew 5:30). May the Lord give us the courage to cut from our lives that which keeps us from abundant living in Him.

Lord, give me the wisdom to make adjustments in my life. Help me to put off habits that are destructive. Give me the courage to say no when evil knocks at the door.

Loyalty

Many a man proclaims his own loyalty, but a faithful man who can find? (Proverbs 20:6).

Cats and dogs are proverbial enemies. The comic strip, *Garfield*, always portrays the cat teasing and taunting big dogs, especially if they are chained up. In real life, though, you will occasionally find a dog and a cat that defy the odds and become good friends. This was the case of a beautiful German shepherd dog we once owned. He and our cat slowly developed not a tolerance for each other, but a close relationship. One evening our dog had meandered out on the road that runs in front of our country place. Unfortunately, he was hit by a car, but he had enough strength and determination to crawl back to our porch doorway and lay down. There he died, but early the next morning when we went to the doorway, we saw not only the lifeless body of our German shepherd, but our cat lying beside him, keeping a lonely vigil. To me this was a demonstration of animal loyalty.

The Canadian geese I have raised have also exemplified the virtue of loyalty to each other and their offspring. For many years, I had a large gander with a broken wing. He mated a female that could fly. She would frequently take to the airways but would always come back to my small pond surrounded by woods. When autumn came and the wild geese honked on their southern flight, I'm sure she was tempted to follow them. But rather than enjoying the freedom of the boundless sky, she chose to remain with her crippled mate. As these two geese raised their families, they swam in formation. The gander led with the goslings in a line behind him. The female brought up the rear, thus giving protection in front and back. I read about an unseasonably late spring snowstorm in Alaska that came upon the breeding ground of Canadian geese. The snow continued to a depth of three feet. Days

later, as the snow melted away, an amazing picture of protection was revealed. Scores of dead geese were still on their nests. They had chosen to suffocate rather than leave the eggs they were protecting.

One of the great incidents of loyalty in Scripture is that of Daniel. He was a young Hebrew boy with tremendous potential. He was taken into captivity in Babylon during the exile. There he was trained for a leadership position in the government of King Darius. However, as so often happens, some Babylonian officials were envious of the young Hebrew's growing popularity. Therefore, they plotted to entrap him. They knew that Daniel prayed regularly to his God. These plotters prevailed on Darius to publish an edict that worship must be offered to no god or person but to the monarch alone, and that when Darius drove forth in his chariot, all persons of every rank and station were to prostrate themselves before him. The penalty for refusing to worship the monarch was death at the hands of hungry lions.

On a quiet night, Daniel could hear the hoarse roars of the lions as they paced back and forth in their cages. But Daniel did not have to worry about his decision. It had been made long before, when he had decided to always be faithful to his God—no matter what would happen. So Daniel did not change his devotional routine. He did not close his western windows facing Jerusalem. He continued to pray (and be seen), leaving the issue in God's hands. Daniel received a reprieve from God when he was thrown into the lions' den as their mouths were closed. In this case, loyalty was rewarded by life. Sometimes, the end is death in this life, but an eternal reward in heaven.

A Spanish scholar wrote, "Culture survives when it receives a constant flow of vitality from those who practice it." Think of those words, "flow of vitality from those who practice it." Christianity survives, not from those who just talk about it, but from those who actually practice it. Loyalty and faithfulness to God must be demonstrated in deeds. In frustration over the lack of true loyalty, the writer of Proverbs said, "Many a man proclaims his own loyalty, but a faithful man who can find?"

Lord, may I declare my dependence and my allegiance to you every day. Thank you that you are always faithful, so I can count on you. May I be faithful to all those with whom I live.

Coming Home

I will arise and go to my father (Luke 15:18).

One early spring, I purchased four young adult wild Canadian honkers from a farmer who raised geese near the Devil's Lake area of North Dakota. To prevent them from flying away when I released them in our pond, the feathers on one wing of each bird were clipped back several inches. It was a joy to watch these magnificent birds maneuver on the water. They were symbols of grace and power. Frequently, they flapped their wings only to discover that the imbalance created by the clipping of one wing made it impossible to get airborne. I fed them well by supplementing the natural food in the pond with generous amounts of corn. They were also well protected from predators by the four-foot fence that was built surrounding their area.

As the summer progressed I discovered an oversight I had made. New wing feathers grew back in the molting process. Soon, my four geese began short flights across the pond and their wing muscles steadily increased in strength. When the summer days slipped into early autumn, flocks of migrating wild geese flew overhead and honked a clamorous invitation to join them. My geese would cock their heads and wistfully look at their cousins in the trackless sky. The sight and sound stirred a deep longing in their breasts.

Then one day, when I went out to feed the geese, they were no longer there. Disappointment spread across my mind. My project of raising Canadian geese had come to an abrupt end. The pond had an imaginary vacant sign posted on its banks.

The days went by and the October duck and goose-hunting season arrived. I began to wonder whether the geese I had raised would survive the army of hunters filling the air with gun shots aimed at any passing migratory fowl.

One Sunday afternoon, after hearing a goose honking, I went down to our pond and was surprised to see three of my geese had returned. The gander had a broken wing, one female was mortally wounded, and the third was in good condition. The fourth goose was later found dead in the field about thirty yards from the water.

My geese must have flown into the combat zone and did not escape the hostile fire of the hunters. The gander had only a wing shot and evidently the pressure exerted when landing on the pond caused the wing to snap. However, he lived for many years and mated the surviving female, and the two produced many offspring.

The question that lurked in my mind was: why did they come back to the confines of the pond after they had experienced the freedom to fly to regions unknown? One answer seemed most reasonable. Our pond, where there was protection and provision, had become their home. When they discovered the dangers of the world into which they flew, they determined that home was worth coming back to.

There is the well-known story of Scripture about a young boy who left his home in pursuit of the pleasures of the world. He squandered the inheritance given him in advance by his father. His world crumbled around him as the empty promises of passion and pleasure produced only despair and despondency. The bullets of selfishness and sensuality figuratively shot him down. In his hopeless state, thoughts of home flooded his mind, and he knew that is where he belonged. So a contrite, broken boy went back home and experienced the restoring love of a father who was waiting with outstretched arms. It was the best trip he had ever made.

Make your community, church, and family a place that is worth coming back to. The greatest homing instinct, of course, is that God is my home. "Lord, thou hast been our dwelling place in all generations. Before the mountains were brought forth, or ever thou hadst formed the earth and the world, from everlasting to everlasting thou art God" (Psalm 90:1-2).

Thank you, Lord, that you are more willing to forgive than we are to receive forgiveness. Thank you that the door to your kingdom is open for all who are willing to enter. When we are with you, we are really back home where we belong.

Keeping Focused

But one thing I do, forgetting what lies behind and straining forward to what lies ahead, I press on toward the goal for the prize of the upward call of God in Christ Jesus (Philippians 3:13-14).

It was a cool autumn day in north central South Dakota. A few fields of unpicked corn and sunflowers graced the landscape. There were plots of stubble left over from the combine that had harvested the small grain. Large acreages of tall grass were also found in abundance. This, indeed, was pheasant country!

Such was the setting for a good trial run of hunting experience for my young Labrador dog. She was trained well in retrieving a thrown ball. Now was the time to transfer this ability to flush up pheasants and retrieve them when shot down. We were hunting with a more mature Labrador that belonged to my eldest son, Barak. I hoped his dog would serve as a good mentor. My dog witnessed my son's dog retrieve a couple birds. Soon she was getting "the hang of it" and seemed to know what pheasant hunting was all about. I knocked down a bird as it flew over a large pond of water. She lunged into the water, swam to the downed pheasant, and brought it back to shore. I stroked my dog in appreciation for her fine effort.

A little later, while walking through some slough grass on the edge of another pond, up jumped a startled doe and her fawn. My dog did not see these two deer spring from their hiding place, since the giant cattails and swamp grass were very tall. However, she caught the scent and away she went, sniffing the ground, hot on their trail. I called for her to come back, but it was to no avail. Over the distant hills she ran. Much time elapsed before my dog came back, breathless from a futile chase.

The dog was young, and I suppose I needed to have more patience than I demonstrated at that time. It was natural for her to want to chase anything that crossed her path, whether it was a rabbit, a field mouse, or another bird. The goal, however, was to teach her to focus on the object of the hunt, which was the ring neck pheasant. If she continued running after every creature that caught her attention, she would fail as a hunting dog. She would miss the duty for which she was bred.

In the field of sports the coach is always emphasizing to his players the importance of focusing on the game. Attention is so easily diverted. There are lapses in concentration and soon the game is lost.

Christians are constantly tempted to stray from the original purpose of walking in the footsteps of Christ. They start out on the right trail, but occasionally stray from that path. Apparently that is what happened to one of apostle Paul's companions. Paul wrote, "For Demas, in love with the present world, has deserted me" (II Timothy 4:10). The scent of wealth, power, prestige, and pleasure may beckon us to lose our first loyalty, which is to Christ.

Therefore, in our earthly walk, we must learn the art of concentrated endeavor and the power that comes from focusing our energies on a given task. When you write, you must set aside some other things and concentrate on your composition. If you have some extra pounds, you cannot take them off if you keep nibbling on every delicacy that comes along. If you are going to be a good parent, you must set aside some time and creativity for the family. One of life's greatest temptations is to be diverted into that which is marginal and peripheral, and to miss that which is focal.

The writer of Hebrews summarizes it well: "Therefore, since we are surrounded by so great a cloud of witnesses, let us also lay aside every weight, and sin which clings so closely, and let us run with perseverance that race that is set before us, looking to Jesus the pioneer and perfecter of our faith, who for the joy that was set before him endured the cross, despising the shame and is seated at the right hand of the throne of God" (Hebrews 12:1-2).

Lord, I once read that the chief end of man is to glorify God and enjoy Him forever. Help me to focus on that more consistently.

Needing Each Other

Many were gathered together and were praying (Acts 12:12).

Spring and fall are seasons that often find my gaze focused heavenward. The sky becomes a place of increased activity as the migrating birds begin flocking together mapping out their itinerary for their northern and southern flights. It has always intrigued me as it stirs a restless instinct in my soul. I become aware that I am not a permanent resident of this world, but have a heavenly destination.

Several times each season I have been privileged to watch beautiful trumpeter swans fly overhead in formation. They are like white ghosts floating in the blue sky. The trumpeter swan has a smaller cousin called the whistling swan. Its distinguishing feature is a yellow patch on its bill. The whistling swan is considered the most graceful of all birds on water and in the air. This migratory bird spends its summers in the northern parts of Alaska and Canada and winter on the southern coasts of America.

The whistling swan is a high flyer and can attain an altitude of six thousand feet. At this height it is almost impossible to see a flock going overhead on their migratory flight. The swan also employs the V-formation. While flying in this pattern, the whistling swan has been clocked at speeds up to one hundred miles per hour.

Traveling in the V-formation, a flock of twenty-five birds are able to travel seventy percent farther than one swan flying by itself. The lead swan "breaks the trail" for the others that follow. As each bird flaps its wings it creates an updraft for the bird behind it, thus lessening the air resistance. When the lead goose tires, it drops back in the formation and a new leader takes over. The swans depend on each other to arrive at their destination safely and efficiently.

Another example of nature in interdependence is found in the giant redwood trees of California. They stand so tall and erect as though they can do it alone. However, that is not the case! The redwood tree has a shallow root system so they need to grow in groves where their root systems intertwine. In this way they support each other so they can withstand the stormy gales. If one stands by itself, it would be easily toppled by a strong wind.

God created human beings for community. People need people. John Donne wrote, "No man is an island entire of himself; every man is a piece of the continent, a part of the main . . . If anyone dies it diminishes me for I am involved in humanity."

As a boy I often played along the railroad tracks. My friend and I competed to see who could walk the farthest on a single rail without falling off. Neither of us got too far before losing balance. However, one day we discovered that if each of us got on an opposite rail and extended our hands to balance each other, we could walk almost indefinitely without tumbling off. That which we could not do alone we could do together.

"Doing your own thing" has been a slogan of our times. But the solo adventure must give way to the advance of the whole team. Togetherness rather than solitary greatness is a key concept. It is a total orchestration. The Christian life is not supposed to be a lonely picket, but always walking together in company. Made in the image of God, we are so constituted that we thrive on partnership, companionship, and fellowship. We do things better, are more productive, and are much happier when we are helping each other. Lending a helping hand benefits the receiver as well as the giver. We really do need one another!

The early church grew quickly as they were strengthened by being together. "And they devoted themselves to the apostles' teaching and fellowship, to the breaking of bread, and to prayer" (Acts 2:42).

Thank you, Lord, that I can lean on your everlasting arms. I thank you also for friends on whom I can lean for support and encouragement. I'm glad I don't have to fly solo.

Keep Growing

But grow in the grace and knowledge of our Lord and Savior Jesus Christ (II Peter 3:18).

A few years ago, my wife and I, along with our daughter, Debbie, strolled along the beach of the Pacific Ocean. As the waves lapped against the shore and then receded, the shells of many sea mollusks and urchins came into view. We sorted through some of the unbroken ones in order to bring home a collection of remembrances from the sea. The sand dollar, a flat sea urchin with a petal-like star in the middle, was one of our favorite finds. On this area of the coast they were very prevalent.

Although we found no chambered nautilus shell, to me it has become the sea mollusk which preaches an important sermon on the significance of a lifelong growth. In the spiraling shell of gradually enlarging compartments, this sea creature lives. As it grows it makes another compartment, larger than the last. It moves from one chamber to another until it finally dies and is free, leaving behind its shell.

This little sea creature fascinated one of our famous American jurists and poets, Oliver Wendell Holmes, as it conjured up the imagery of the human soul expanding and growing until someday it, too, would move on. The poem was entitled, *"The Chambered Nautilus."* The last stanza states:

> Build thee more stately mansions, O my soul,
> As the swift seasons roll!
> Leave thy low vaulted past!
> Let each new temple, nobler than the last,
> Shut thee from heaven with a dome more vast,
> Till thou at length are free,
> Leaving thine outgrown shell by life's unresting sea!

In our culture, we endeavor to hold on to youth beyond the boundaries set by the biological clock. Ponce de Leon didn't find the fountain of youth, and neither will we. But we keep on trying. Barbells get pumped, hair is dyed, the face gets stretched, the chin tucked, and breasts get a lift. But we get older, and can't deny it. Even though the muscle tone begins to recede and the agility becomes rigidity, that is no cause for the spirit to stop soaring to new heights. Body age should not determine the growth of mind and spirit. When William James celebrated his seventieth birthday, a friend asked him if he believed in immortality. "Never stronger," he replied, "but more so as I grow older. Because I am just getting fit to live."

General Douglas MacArthur said, "Nobody grows old by merely living a number of years. People grow old by deserting their ideals. Years may wrinkle the skin, but to give up wrinkles the soul."

Functionally, we are somewhat like a bicycle. A bicycle maintains its poise and equilibrium as long as it is going forward. We all get into trouble when we try to maintain our balance sitting still, with no place to go. To keep moving forward is necessary for healthy living.

When Robert Browning lost his beloved wife, Elizabeth, his life was shattered, and for three years it seemingly was on hold. Then he began thinking about the words of a man he had admired for years, the twelfth century scholar Rabbi ben Ezra. He had written about approaching the twilight of life with joy and hope, with eagerness and not gloom. If you keep growing it can be the best of life. Robert Browning began to get hold of himself again and produced great inspiration. In his classic poem, *Rabbi ben Ezra,* he said:

> Grow old along with me!
> The best is yet to be!
> The last of life, for which the first was made.
> Our times are in his hand
> Who saith: "A whole I planned,
> Youth shows but half; trust God; see all, nor be afraid!"

Let us keep growing so expectancy about tomorrow looms larger than nostalgia about yesterday.

Lord, at Pentecost, Peter preached that "old men shall dream dreams." Help me to understand that life can sprout new shoots of adventure at any age. Keep me alive as long as I live.

A Bold Fighter

I have fought the good fight, I have finished the race, I have kept the faith (II Timothy 4:7).

While driving in the lake country of Minnesota in late winter, I saw a small, cylindrical animal scurrying across the gravel road heading toward some tall weeds in a swampy area. I stopped and watched this little creature until it disappeared in the underbrush of the swamp. My first inclination was that it might be a mink, but it was pure white with a black tip on the tail. At home I checked my old biology book and concluded it was a weasel. The weasel is a small mammal measuring seven to fourteen inches in length. In summer, its coat turns dark brown except for a white belly and neck. In the northern winters the coat becomes white providing camouflage against the snow. Wearing its white coat, it also goes by the name ermine.

The weasel's body is like a pipe cleaner, allowing it to track rodents, shrews, and rabbits down their holes. They attempt to corner their prey and then kill them with a bite to the neck. The weasel is a bold, savage hunter. If this small bundle of finely tuned muscles were the size of a Labrador dog, it would be the most vicious animal on earth. Once the weasel is engaged in a conflict, it will persist until its opponent is subdued or it will die fighting. The weasel does not consider retreat as an option.

A larger member of the weasel family is the wolverine. It grows to a weight of thirty-one to sixty pounds and lives in the northern forests and tundra areas. It, too, is a fighter and has earned an unequaled reputation for ferocity by attacking and killing larger animals, such as caribou. The wolverine would rather fight than run.

Suppose Jesus ran for his life on the night of Gethsemane, instead of remaining in the garden to pray and then to die. He could have fled into Galilee and hid with his friends until the whole affair had blown over. But he didn't. He faced the opposition and won the battle against sin, death, and the power of the devil that we might be ransomed and set free.

Church historians often refer to the "church militant" and the "church triumphant." The church militant meant the church on earth as it battles the forces of evil. The church triumphant was the assembly of faithful warriors who had fought the good fight of faith and had been transferred to the heavenly kingdom.

This terminology has largely been set on the shelf today. Some people in the pews wince a bit when we sing hymns like "Onward, Christian Soldiers" or "Fight the Good Fight with All Your Might." They don't like war in any form, and words that conjure up conflict are taboo. There is so much trouble in the world that we want the church to be a tranquil sea, where our little boats may dock safely and serenely.

All this is in sharp contrast to the early church. The recruiting of members was as though they were enlisting in the army. Paul tells Timothy, "Share in suffering as a good soldier of Jesus Christ" (II Timothy 2:3). The call of Christ was the summons of a commander to do battle. The followers of Christ often had to forfeit business opportunities, cut themselves of from social attachment, struggle against the pull of pagan associations. They took a stand against false doctrine and all forms of immorality. They did not run from evil opposition but, with the "sword of the Spirit, which is the word of God," fought against it (Ephesians 6:17).

Lord, I need to ask myself if I truly live like a soldier of the Cross and a faithful follower of the Lamb. Am I afraid to own your cause and blush to speak your name? Increase my courage, Lord!

A Lunar Eclipse

Again Jesus spoke to them, saying, "I am the light of the world; he who follows me will not walk in darkness, but will have the light of life" (John 8:12).

It was a clear, crisp night in January when my wife and I gazed out our bedroom window. A blanket of fluffy white snow covered the ground. On this still winter evening it was a scene of serenity. Viewing through the naked branches of some giant cottonwood tress, we began watching the eclipse of the moon. The shadow of the earth slowly passed across the moon's face, leaving a fainter disc still visible. As the total eclipse approached, the darkened moon face took on a reddish hue. Blood red! We both rushed out the door to take some camera pictures and get a better vantage point for observing the phenomenon of nature. In ancient days this seemingly strange moon happening was interpreted as an evil omen of some type.

Of course it is a natural occurrence when the earth gets directly between the sun and the moon, thus obscuring the reflection of the sun's light of the surface of the moon. The moon, having no light of its own, is darkened.

My mind was now set in motion. The psalmist said, "For the Lord God is a sun and shield . . ." (Psalm 84:10). Again, "This is the message we have heard from him and proclaim to you, that God is light and in him is no darkness at all" (I John 1:5). The moon that has captured the imagination in folklore and stirs the heart with romantic suggestiveness has no light of its own. Rather it reflects the majesty of the sun. Glory belongs to the sun.

Let me interpose a parable. In our dining room there is a large hutch, which displays many pieces of crystal glassware. It is evening and we walk into the room in total darkness. I quickly flick on the light switch and, in the fraction of a second, thousand of reflections reach our eyes from the different cuts of crystal pieces. They have no light in themselves, but as soon as the light is turned on, every one of them leaps at me with a message: "Though we have no light within ourselves we reflect the light that is above us."

When Paul speaks of Moses meeting God on the mountain, he says that when Moses came down it was with "such splendor that the Israelites would not look at Moses' face because of its brightness. . ." (II Corinthians 3:7). What happened? Was it not that Moses was reflecting the glory of God? Paul then indicates that the ministry of righteousness in Christ will have greater glory and splendor.

When you think of the people who have influenced and spiritually enriched your life, it is perhaps because they are reflecting the light of the Lord. They fling back into our world the radiance they get from Him.

So I must ask myself some strategic questions. Am I reflecting the light of Christ or have I become too tarnished or dusty to care? Have I allowed barriers of selfishness, pride or other sins to erect their walls that have shut me off from the Son of Righteousness so the reflection is dimmed? Have I let the world get in between myself and God as the earth gets in between the moon and the sun, thus causing an eclipse?

Such musings happened on a winter night of lunar eclipse. "And we, who with unveiled faces all reflect the Lord's glory. . . (II Corinthians 3:18 NIV).

Lord, shine on us so we may reflect your glory. May our lives mirror your likeness.

The Butterfly Symbol

For the trumpet will sound, and the dead will be raised imperishable,
And we shall be changed (I Corinthians 15:22).

I should like to close this book with a meditational reflection I wrote in Heaven and Nature Sing (Concordia Publishing House—1977).

If you have romped in God's big outdoors and looked for miracles, you have no doubt seen one or more. It was a day when the warm sunshine was beckoning life to come and play in the gentle breezes of the meadow. There was an expectancy that seemed to creep over all creation. Some time prior to this day, a fluffy caterpillar had crawled out on a branch to die. Securing itself, it had spun a silken cocoon like a casket around its total body. Scientifically, we could say it was going through the pupa stage. Something was happening in that woven tomb—death was giving way to new life. If a small boy would have tried for a sneak preview of the action inside, he would have destroyed the miracle. But nobody had interrupted the plan. So the miracle happened. The chrysalis burst open after a violent series of convulsive movements. Out came a beautiful, multicolored butterfly. It moved its wings, caught a draft of air, and soon soared. That which was earthbound as a caterpillar was now free to explore the sky. My heart skipped a beat as I stood and observed the empty caterpillar casket.

Butterflies are beautiful. Once Arthus Brisbane, a well-known newspaper editor of some years ago, told a tale of some caterpillars pulling an empty cocoon to its burial place. The caterpillars were dressed in black and weeping sadly. While they were on the long, somber journey, a butterfly was floating above them. While they wept, the butterfly was rejoicing in his newfound freedom and life.

What a transformation! That which seemed like a sealed tomb became a doorway to exhilarating life. This surely speaks to an instinct that God placed in my soul. "He has made everything beautiful; also he has put eternity into man's mind" (Ecclesiasties 3:11). My casket shall not be a dead end for me. The casket has been conquered. Jesus, who came back from the tomb, says, "I am the resurrection and the life; he who believes in me, though he die, yet shall he live, and whoever believes in me shall never die" (John 11:25-26). He demonstrated this that first Easter morning when he walked out of Joseph's sepulcher and started stepping down through the centuries with the good news of salvation and life.

Do you wonder what it will be like in the world beyond? We have no clues of the furnishing of heaven except that it will be beyond compare. "What no eye has seen, nor ear heard, nor the heart of man conceived, what God has prepared for those who love him" (I Corinthians 2:9). Even though Scripture indicates we will be recognizable people as we are now, the glory of the imperishable nature will be a transformation as superb as the magnificent metamorphosis of the butterfly. Benjamin Franklin, who died in 1790, wrote this epitaph:

> The body of Franklin Printer
> Like the cover of an old book
> Its contents torn out
> And stript of lettering and guilding
> Lies here. Food for worms.
> But the work shall not be lost.
> For it will appear once more,
> In a new and more elegant edition,
> Revised and corrected by the Author.

In the meantime, we can deliberately and patiently spin a cocoon of the threads of love and service to others around the days of our lives. For we know that "in the Lord your labor is not in vain" (I Corinthians 15:58).

Lord, thank you that you are not through with me at the time of my death. It is good to know that you will bring to completion all that you have started. In the meantime, strengthen my wings of hope that I might fly free in your grace and promise.